EDITOR: LEE JOHNSON

OSPREY MILITARY **ELITE SERIES** 50

THE PRAETORIAN GUARD

Text by
DR BORIS RANKOV
Colour plates by
RICHARD HOOK

First published in Great Britain in 1994 by
Osprey, an imprint of Reed Consumer Books Limited
Michelin House, 81 Fulham Road,
London SW3 6RB
and Auckland, Melbourne, Singapore and Toronto

© Copyright 1994 Reed International Books Limited

ISBN 1 85532 361 3

Filmset in Great Britain by Keyspools Ltd, Golborne,
Lancashire
Printed through Bookbuilders Ltd, Hong Kong

Acknowledgements

The author wishes to express his thanks to the
institutions which provided photographs for this
volume: the National Museum of Antiquities of
Scotland, Edinburgh; the Ashmolean Museum,
Oxford; the Museum of London; the British Museum;
and especially the German Archaeological Institute,
Rome. I should also like to thank the artist, Richard
Hook, for his cheerful patience in altering the colour
plates specification every time I changed my mind; and
to my wife, Kati, who drew the map, and lived with
the Guard much longer than it was reasonable to
expect of her.

Artist's note

Readers may care to note that the original paintings
from which the colour plates in this book were
prepared are available for private sale. All
reproduction copyright whatsoever is retained by the
publisher. All enquiries should be addressed to:

Scorpio Gallery
PO Box 475
Hailsham
E. Sussex BN27 2SL

The publishers regret that they can enter into no
correspondence upon this matter.

Publisher's note

Readers may wish to study this title in conjunction
with the following Osprey publications:

MAA 46 *The Roman Army from Caesar to Trajan*
MAA 93 *The Roman Army from Hadrian to
Constantine*
MAA 129 *Rome's Enemies (1) Germanics and
Dacians*

For a catalogue of all books published by Osprey Military
please write to:

**The Marketing Manager,
Consumer Catalogue Department,
Osprey Publishing Ltd,
Michelin House, 81 Fulham Road,
London SW3 6RB**

THE PRAETORIAN GUARD

INTRODUCTION

The Praetorian Guard have become a byword for any military force which is used to prop up a ruthless regime. There is no doubt that they performed this function in the Roman Empire. As the main body of troops in Rome they were the emperor's instrument to discourage plotting and rebellion and to crush unrest. They were the emperor's most immediate line of defence; they could also, on occasion, be his most deadly enemies.

Throughout their history the Guard were all too aware that they could make or destroy emperors as they wished. And yet, when they did so it was almost always for their own selfish and immediate reasons rather than out of any wider political conviction or need. Numerous Prefects of the Guard intrigued and fought for power, but the mass of the Guard tended to stay neutral unless their own interests were directly involved.

Comfortable and relatively safe in their barracks in Rome, enjoying shorter service and better pay and bonuses than any other unit in the Empire, and often involved in nothing more arduous than sentry-duty at the palace, the Praetorians were the envy of the legionaries stationed at the frontiers. All this might seem an unlikely background for an elite fighting unit; yet when the Guard did take the field, they appear to have been well enough trained and officered to acquit themselves well. Indeed, in the late 1st and 2nd centuries, when emperors frequently campaigned in person and took the Guard with them, they proved both efficient and loyal.

Despite the importance of the Praetorians both politically and as a military unit, relatively little has been written about them. The effect has been that the

Augustus (27 BC–AD 14), Rome's first emperor, who kept on his Praetorian Cohorts from the period of the civil wars and so created an imperial guard. In 2 BC he placed the individual cohorts and their tribunes under the overall command of two Roman knights with the title of Prefect. Cast of the statue from Prima Porta in the Museo della Civiltà Romana, Rome.

extent of their involvement on the battlefields of the Empire has been underestimated, and that they have sometimes been perceived as a ceremonial unit, equipped with archaic armour designed for show. This can now be shown to be incorrect. The principal works on the Guard remain Marcel Durry's *Les cohortes prétoriennes* in French, published in 1938, and Alfredo Passerini's *Le coorti pretorie* in Italian, published in 1939; the impact of both on the present work has been considerable. There has been no monograph in English before this volume. Although the emphasis here is firmly on the appearance of the Guard, the bibliography at the end of this text should allow those interested in finding out more about the Praetorians in general to satisfy their curiosity.

ORIGINS OF THE GUARD

The Praetorian Cohorts, collectively known to us as the Praetorian Guard, are often thought of as the innovation of Rome's first emperor, Augustus. This is not the case, since such cohorts are known to have served generals in the late Republic. The term could be used quite informally, to refer to the group (*cohors*) of friends and companions accompanying a Roman commander or governor (*praetor* was the original title of the consuls who were supreme commanders in the field). But by the late 1st century BC it is clear that it could mean a select unit of troops acting as a bodyguard. This was quite possibly a development of the Civil War period.

By the late 40s BC both Octavian (the future Augustus) and his rival Antony were operating with a number of individually organised Praetorian units. Appian says that they divided between them 8,000 veterans who were formed into cohorts. Antony took three cohorts to the East with him and in 32 BC issued a coin in honour of his Praetorians. According to Orosius, Octavian had five cohorts at Actium.

After his victory, Octavian amalgamated his force with those of his opponent in a symbolic reunification of Julius Caesar's army. With his own praetorians and those of Antony, he will already have had the administrative basis for a permanent Guard. By 13 BC Augustus, as he now was, had established

The Emperor Tiberius (AD 14–37), who allowed his Praetorian Prefect Sejanus to concentrate the Guard in the purpose-built Praetorian Camp in AD 23, and thus became the Praetorians' second founder. Tiberius' birth-sign, Scorpio, was adopted as the emblem of the Guard. Museo Archeologico, Venice. (German Archaeological Institute)

the length of service in the Guard as 12 years as opposed to the normal 16 in the legions, but in 5 BC, Tacitus says this had to be increased to 16 and 20 years respectively.

We do not know how many cohorts Octavian kept on, although inscriptions suggest that there were initially nine, which is also the number attested by Tacitus for AD 23. Nor do we know the size of the individual Praetorian Cohorts, though one might guess at about 500 men, as in the regular legions. What we do know from Suetonius is that during Augustus' reign he was careful to have only three cohorts based in Rome itself, and these were not in a camp but billeted around the city; the others were scattered round the towns of Italy. It is clear that Augustus was extremely wary of flaunting too blatantly the basis of his power.

Until 2 BC, each Praetorian Cohort was an independent unit under the separate command of a tribune of equestrian rank (i.e. a Roman knight). At that point Augustus appointed two senior Roman knights to take overall command as Praetorian

Prefects. Whilst in Rome their principal duty was to mount guard at Augustus' home on the Palatine. Each afternoon, at the eighth hour, the tribune of the cohort on duty would receive the watchword from the emperor in person. After the construction of the Praetorian Camp in AD 23 there was a tribune on duty there as well. Other duties included escorting the emperor and other members of the imperial family, and, if necessary, acting as a form of riot police. Again, to avoid antagonising the population of Rome and in accordance with Republican custom, the Praetorians did not wear armour when performing such duties within the city. Instead they wore the rather formal toga, which would still make them conspicuous in a crowd but was a civilian garment and the mark of a Roman citizen (Martial *Epigrams* VI 76; Tacitus *Annals* XVI 27; *Histories* I 38). Even military displays were infrequent, and the troops appeared in armour in Rome only on very special occasions (Tacitus *Annals* XII 36; Suetonius *Nero* 13; Dio LXIII 4).

A recently discovered inscription suggests that towards the end of Augustus' reign, the number of cohorts rose to 12 for a brief period. This inscription (Letta = *AE* 1978 no. 286) records a man who was, unusually, tribune of two cohorts in succession: the Eleventh, apparently at the end of Augustus' reign, and the Fourth at the beginning of Tiberius'. According to Tacitus there were only nine cohorts by AD 23. The three Urban Cohorts, which were numbered consecutively after the Praetorians, were raised around the end of Augustus' reign, so it seems likely that the last three Praetorian Cohorts were simply redesignated. At any rate, we know from inscriptions that the Praetorians were back up to 12 cohorts by the reign of Caligula (AD 37–41) or Claudius (AD 41–54).

It was at this period that the Guard took the field in earnest for the first time. On the death of Augustus in AD 14 his successor Tiberius was faced with mutinies amongst both the Rhine and the Pannonian armies, who were complaining about their conditions of service, especially in comparison with those of the Praetorians. The Pannonian forces were dealt with by Tiberius' son Drusus, accompanied by two Praetorian Cohorts, Praetorian cavalry, and the German Bodyguard (see below). The German mutiny was put down by Tiberius' stepson and intended heir Ger-

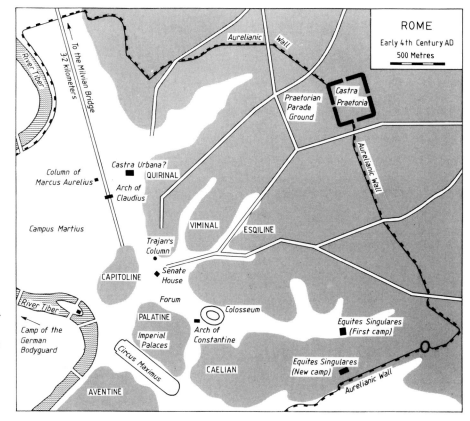

Map of Rome in the early 4th century AD (after Durry), showing the situation of Praetorian Camp and of the camps of the German Bodyguard and the Equites Singulares Augusti, the line of the Aurelianic Walls of AD 271, and the sites of the principal monuments relating to the Guard.

5

A model of the Praetorian Camp in the early 4th century, viewed from the south. The 1st century brick walls, heightened and incorporated into the 3rd century defences of Rome, are mostly still standing and now enclose the modern garrison of Rome. The internal layout is largely conjectural, based partly on references to buildings on inscriptions and even on depictions on coins, although there are archaeological traces of two-storey barracks and of rooms ranged round the inside face of the perimeter wall. Model in the Museo della Civiltà Romana, Rome. (German Archaeological Institute)

manicus, who then led the legions and detachments of the Guard in an invasion of Germany which continued over the next two years.

More significant than the growth in the number of cohorts or the Guard's first proper campaign, however, was the rise to prominence of Lucius Aelius Seianus (Sejanus), the first of many prefects to use the post to further his own ambitions. He concentrated under his regime all the Praetorian Cohorts in the new camp on the Viminal Hill in Rome. Sejanus had been joint prefect with his father under Augustus and then sole prefect from AD 15. He used the position to make himself indispensable to the new emperor, who was unable to persuade the Senate to share the burden of running the Empire. Sejanus found, however, that he had alienated Tiberius' son Drusus, and when the heir to the throne, Germanicus, died in AD 19, he was understandably afraid that Drusus would be the next emperor. He therefore poisoned Drusus with the aid of the latter's wife, and embarked on a ruthless programme of eliminating all rivals and persuading Tiberius to make him his heir. He came very close to succeeding, but his plotting was revealed in AD 31 and he was killed.

As part of the consolidation of his own position Sejanus persuaded Tiberius to build the Praetorian Camp and to concentrate the Guard. Tiberius thus became, in effect, the second founder of the Praetorians, and it is almost certainly because of this that they adopted Tiberius' birth-sign, Scorpio, as their particular emblem.

The Praetorian Camp (*Castra Praetoria*)

The walls of the camp built for the Praetorians in AD 23 can still be seen in Rome today. The remaining northern, eastern and southern walls stand on the Viminal Hill where they house the modern-day garrison of Rome (the western wall, inside the circuit of the Aurelianic Wall, was destroyed by Constantine in AD 312). They enclose an area of just over 17 hectares, about two-thirds the size of the average legionary fortress on the frontiers. This suggests a capacity of something like 4,000 men; but the few internal buildings which can be traced include extra rooms ranged round the inside of the walls and traces of two-storey barracks, neither of which can be found in any legionary fortress. A true capacity of 12,000 men or more may therefore not be fanciful.

Tiberius' walls, built of concrete with a red-brick facing, were some 3.5 metres high. The line of the rampart walk can still be seen, as can the original crenellations and the sites of towers and gates on the northern and eastern walls. The walls were damaged in the Civil War of AD 69 and repaired by Vespasian (AD 69–79). The wall then underwent no major changes until the early 3rd century, when it was heightened, perhaps by Caracalla (AD 211–17); and subsequently repaired with heightened towers after

The north wall of the Praetorian Camp as it is today. The horizontal moulding half-way up the picture marks the level of the original Tiberian walkway, and above it, clearly visible, is the line of the contemporary parapets. Further up are the parapets of the extension made when the Camp was incorporated into the Aurelianic City walls in 271. At the very top are the remains of a final extension made in the early 4th century, probably by the Emperor Maxentius.

the sieges of AD 238. In 271 the Emperor Aurelian ringed Rome with the impressive walls which still survive and bear his name, and he incorporated the Praetorian Camp into them. This involved raising the height of the curtain wall almost to that of the towers of AD 238 and adding new battlements and towers. Then, in about 310, the Emperor Maxentius made a final heightening with new parapets in anticipation of a siege of the city by his rivals. This failed to save him, and when Constantine took the city after the Battle of the Milvian Bridge in 312 he emphasised the disbanding of the Guard by demolishing the inner wall of their camp.

ORGANISATION

As we have seen, Augustus seems to have begun with nine Praetorian Cohorts, increased the number to 12 in the latter part of his reign, and reduced it to nine again by redesignating three as Urban Cohorts in about AD 12. This according to Tacitus was the number in AD 23 when Sejanus concentrated them into the Praetorian Camp. Inscriptions show that they were back up to 12 by the reign of Gaius Caligula (AD 37–41) or Claudius (AD 41–54). Vitellius briefly formed 16 new cohorts after dismissing the old ones in AD 69, but Vespasian had brought them back down to nine by AD 76 at the latest. Finally, Vespasian's son Domitian (AD 81–96) increased the number to ten, at which strength they remained until finally disbanded by Constantine. From the year 2 BC the Guard was under the overall control of two or even one prefect, but the individual cohorts continued to be organised independently, each with a tribune at its head. The tribunes had as their immediate subordinates a senior centurion entitled *trecenarius* and a number of ordinary centurions of equal rank; each of these led a century of 80 men.

The size of the cohorts has always been disputed, and it is likely that it varied over time. There is no evidence for the early period, but if they were of the same size as legionary cohorts then they would be about 500 strong and organised in six centuries of 80 men each. Tacitus tells us that Vitellius' new cohorts were 1,000 strong (which may actually mean ten centuries of 80 men each, like the first cohort of each legion in the period immediately after). Dio anachronistically attributes 10,000 men in ten cohorts to Augustus' Guard, but may be extrapolating back from his own time in the later 2nd century AD. Calculations from inscribed discharge lists roughly accord with this figure, and suggest an increase in size to about 1,500 (perhaps a doubling from 800, presumably organised in 20 centuries) under Commodus in AD 187/8 or Septimius Severus (AD 193–211). This would be in line with the likely figure for Urban Cohorts in Dio's time. These figures would give an overall size of the Guard of 4,500–6,000 men under Augustus, 12,800 under Vitellius, 7,200 under Vespasian, 8,000 from Domitian to Commodus or Severus, and 15,000 thereafter.

The great majority of these men were infantry, but, as with the legions, the Guard did include an attachment of cavalry. Inscriptions suggest that men could become cavalry (*equites*) after about five years' service as infantry. Such men remained on the books of their original centuries but operated together in *turmae* of 30 men each commanded by an *optio equitum*. One inscription (*CIL* VI 32638) suggests a proportion of one *turma* to two centuries – i.e. three *turmae* per cohort in the Augustan period, five per cohort in the late 1st and 2nd centuries, and ten per cohort in the 3rd century. Inscriptions which mention a *vexillarius equitum* (cavalry flag-bearer) indicate that their standard was a *vexillum* or flag.

The Guard also had a special elite cavalry section, known as the *speculatores Augusti*, who formed the emperor's cavalry bodyguard. Individually these men remained on the books of their own centuries and cohorts, but collectively they formed a separate corps. They were apparently distinguished by a special form of boot of unknown form, the *caliga speculatoria* (Suetonius *Caligula* 52); and they received special honorific bronze diplomas on discharge. The strength of this body of men is uncertain, but they had their own riding instructor (*exercitator*) and were commanded by a *centurio speculatorum*.

Service in the Praetorian Cohorts

Service in the Praetorian Guard was in many ways an attractive proposition, offering a shorter period of service and better pay than the legions, together with the advantages of living in Rome, and less frequent exposure to danger and discomfort. We know from inscriptions that men were recruited between the ages of 15 and 32, a rather broader spread than for legionary recruitment, which was usually between 18 and 23. In the reign of Vitellius (AD 69) and from the reign of Septimius Severus (AD 193–211) onwards, men are also known to have been transferred to the Guard from the *Vigiles, the Cohortes Urbanae*, and the legions. This became the normal method of recruitment in the 3rd century.

Tacitus says that in the reign of Tiberius (AD 14–37) Praetorians were recruited mainly from Etruria, Umbria and Latium; and Dio, that before the reform of Septimius Severus (AD 193–211) Praetorians came only from Italy, Spain, Macedonia and Noricum (modern Austria). Inscriptions confirm that most came from central and northern Italy and the areas cited by Dio in the first two centuries AD. At this period, therefore, the Guard tended to be drawn from the most prosperous and Romanised parts of the Empire. When Septimius Severus came to power, however, he dismissed the unruly Praetorians who had tried to buy and sell the Empire in 193, and replaced them with men from his own Danubian legions. After this, Italians were no longer recruited at all; instead it was mostly men from the less Romanised Danube region who served in the Guard, after four to nine years' service in the legions.

From 5 BC onwards, Praetorians signed up for 16 years' service, compared with the 20 years demanded in the Urban Cohorts and the 25 years in the legions. When men were transferred in, they only had to serve the balance of 16 years. In 27 BC Augustus established the pay of Praetorians as double that of legionaries. By AD 14 they were receiving 720 denarii per year, three times the 225 of the legionaries; this differential is likely to have remained constant throughout the history of the Guard. Tiberius gave the Praetorians a cash bonus (*donativum*) of 1,000 denarii after the fall of Sejanus in AD 31; Claudius gave them five years' salary at his accession, becoming the first emperor to buy their loyalty in this way, according to Suetonius. Most emperors followed suit to a greater or lesser extent while at the same time the legions often got nothing. Such slender evidence as exists also suggests that Praetorians were more likely to be decorated for courage in battle than legionaries. On retirement they received proportionally larger discharge bonuses, 5,000 as opposed to 3,000 denarii, and, unlike legionaries, they were presented with honorific diplomas on bronze which made legitimate their first marriages and the children born of them (soldiers were not allowed legally to marry before the reign of Septimius Severus). The huge discrepancy in the treatment of Praetorians and of legionaries was obviously the result of their constant presence in Rome and their ability to create and destroy emperors.

In order to be accepted into the Guard and reap these rewards, a man would need to be physically fit, of good character and respectable family. He would also have to make use of all the patronage available, by obtaining letters of recommendation from any men of importance he knew. If he passed the induction procedure and became *probatus*, he would be assigned as a *miles* to one of the centuries of a cohort. After a few years, providing he could gain the attention of his officers by influence or merit, he might obtain a post as an *immunis*, perhaps as a headquarters clerk or a technician, any of which would free him from normal fatigues. A few more years' service might advance him to *principalis*, with double pay, in charge of passing on the watchword (*tesserarius*) or as centurion's deputy (*optio*) or standard-bearer (*signifer*) in the century; or, if highly literate and numerate, he might be appointed to the Prefect's staff.

Only a small number of soldiers would achieve the grade of *principalis*, but those who did might, on completion of their service, be appointed *evocati Augusti* by the emperor. This appointment enabled them to take up administrative, technical or instructor posts in Rome, or a centurionate in a legion, and so extend their careers. Alternatively, some *principales* might before the end of their service be advanced to the rank of centurion in the Guard. The centurionate was enormously prestigious and well

A so-called diploma, or discharge document, issued by the Emperor Philip the Arab to Nebus Tullius of the Fifth Praetorian Cohort from Aelia Mursa (Osijek) on 7 January AD 246. These documents, consisting of two inscribed sheets of bronze sealed together, were given to Praetorians and auxiliaries (but not, curiously, to legionaries) to mark the honourable completion of their period of service. They were mainly honorary, but they also recorded the legitimisation of the first marriage contracted by the recipient whilst serving (which was technically illegal), and of any children born of it. (The Trustees of the British Museum)

paid, and we know that some Roman knights gave up their equestrian status in order to obtain a direct commission to this rank. For the man who had risen to this position it would probably be the culmination of his career, and although there was no restriction on the length of service, he would probably retire in it. Any man who wished to climb further up the ladder would have to transfer to a legion, and very few would be able to do this.

The tribunes at the head of the individual cohorts were Roman knights. Unlike many of the senior officers of the Roman army who were born with equestrian rank, the tribunes usually began their careers in the ranks of the Guard and rose from there. Having first become centurions, they would then have gone on to serve as senior centurions in one or more legions, rising to become *primus pilus* or top centurion in a legion for a period of one year. Returning to Rome after this, they would in succession have held a tribunate in the *Vigiles* (the city's fire-brigade), the tribunate of an Urban Cohort (the para-military police), and finally a tribunate of the Guard. Many other paths to the tribunate were possible, however, including previous service entirely in the legions up to *primus pilus* before the move to Rome. Nevertheless, all tribunes would have been veterans with considerable military experience. Each of the tribunates at Rome would last for a year, after which some men would retire. A few, however, representing the very tip of a huge promotion pyramid, might progress to a second legionary primipilate and thence to the upper echelons of the equestrian career.

A tiny minority of these might even rise to become Praetorian Prefect. Most prefects, however, were men of equestrian birth who had followed a different path. The men who attained command of the Guard after 2 BC were Roman knights of the highest seniority, ranking second only to the Prefects of Egypt. From the time of Vespasian (AD 69–79), whose son Titus held the Praetorian Prefecture himself, they ranked first, and the one or two prefects in post were always amongst the most influential men in the Empire.

THE JULIO-CLAUDIANS

(Sources: Josephus *Jewish Antiquities* XVIII–XX; Tacitus *Annals* XI–XVI; *Histories* I–III; Plutarch *Lives* of Galba, Otho; Suetonius *Lives* of Caligula, Claudius, Nero, Galba, Otho, Vitellius and Vespasian; Cassius Dio LIX–LXIV)

Tiberius' successor was the unhinged megalomaniac Gaius Caligula (AD 37–41), who came to the throne with the aid of Sejanus' successor as Praetorian Prefect, Quintus Sutorius Macro. Caligula's follies supposedly included leading the Guard in triumph on a bridge of boats spanning the Bay of Naples, and taking the Praetorian cavalry on a farcical raid across the Rhine. In 41, it was the sheer disgust and hostility that he had engendered in a tough Praetorian tribune by the name of Cassius Chaerea – whom he teased

The Emperor Claudius (AD 41–54); he was the first emperor to be placed on the throne by the Guard – after he had been found hiding behind a curtain in the palace following the assassination of his nephew Gaius Caligula. He took the Praetorians with him on his invasion of Britain in AD 43. Vatican Museum. (German Archaeological Institute)

mercilessly about his squeaky voice – which led to Caligula's assassination by officers of the Guard. The German Bodyguard (see below) went on the rampage searching for the murderers, whilst the Senate deliberated on the restoration of a Republic. While the Praetorians were looting the Palace in the confusion they came across Caligula's uncle Claudius hiding behind a curtain. In need of an emperor to justify their own existence, they took him off to the Praetorian Camp and proclaimed his accession. The Senate were forced to accede to this coup: the Praetorians' first attempt at king-making had succeeded. Claudius rewarded the Guard with, an unsurprising but generous bonus of five years' salary. Inscriptions reveal that he also took them with him to witness the conclusion of his invasion of Britain in AD 43; and also that it was either Caligula or, more likely, Claudius who brought the number of Praetorian Cohorts back up to twelve.

Nevertheless, when Claudius was poisoned by his wife Agrippina and stepson Nero the Guard were not slow to transfer their allegiance and ensure the latter's accession. Once again a Praetorian Prefect, Sextus Afranius Burrus, wielded enormous influence, this time to the good. After Burrus' death, however, the mounting catalogue of Nero's crimes, which included matricide, again provoked revulsion among the conservative officers of the Guard, and a number of them, including one of Burrus' two successors in the prefecture, were involved in the dangerous Pisonian conspiracy of AD 65. The other Prefect, Tigellinus, took the lead in the suppression of the conspiracy, and the Guard was rewarded with a bonus of 500 denarii per man. Despite this, three years later Tigellinus' new colleague Nymphidius Sabinus saw to it that the Guard deserted Nero in favour of the pretender Galba. Sabinus had promised the Guard 7,500 denarii per man for their loyalty, but Galba had refused to pay. This allowed his rival Otho to bribe 23 *speculatores* of the Guard to proclaim him emperor. Despite the opposition of the cohort on duty at the palace Otho eventually won over the rest of the Guard, and as a result Galba was lynched on 15 January 69.

Under the Julio-Claudian emperors the Guard continued to develop its political role in the most dangerous way possible, but saw little action in the field. However this all changed following the death of Nero. In the 'Year of the Four Emperors' which followed, the Praetorians were engaged in major campaigning for the first time in a century of their existence. Even before Galba's, somewhat brutal, death the governor of Lower Germany, Aulus Vitellius, had been confidently proclaimed emperor by the German armies and was marching toward Rome. Otho, backed by the Praetorians and the armies of the Danube, quickly blocked Vitellius' advance at Bedriacum near Cremona in northern Italy, but was convincingly defeated, partly as a result of the indiscipline of the Praetorians. Rather than cause more bloodshed, or perhaps rather than be lynched like his predecessor, Otho committed suicide on 16 April 69.

Vitellius took his revenge on the Praetorians by executing their centurions and disbanding the existing cohorts. He then created 16 new cohorts, each 1,000 strong, recruited from the legionaries and auxiliaries of his own army. The disbanded Praetorians departed to become the backbone of the army of a new pretender to the throne, Titus Flavius Vespasianus, who was also supported by the armies of the East. After a second terrible battle at Bedriacum Vespasian's forces laid siege to Rome and, led by Otho's former guardsmen, attacked the Praetorian Camp. Vitellius was captured and killed on 20 December 69, and the civil war ended.

The German Bodyguard (*Germani Corporis Custodes*)[1]

For the 1st century of the Principate, the Julio-Claudian emperors had a personal bodyguard of German troops operating alongside the Praetorians. Their origin lay in the period of the civil wars, when foreign mercenaries seem to have been regarded as more reliable than a guard of Roman citizens whose loyalties might be divided. Suetonius tells us that Octavian had maintained a bodyguard of Calgurritani from Spain, which he dismissed after the defeat of Mark Antony in 30 BC; he then kept a guard of Germans until the Varian disaster of AD 9, in which three legions were wiped out in Germany. They were temporarily removed from Rome; but in AD 14 Augustus' successor Tiberius was able to send the Germans with the Praetorian cavalry to help his son Drusus put down a revolt in Pannonia.

[1] See Bellen, 1981.

Unlike the Praetorians, the Germans (*Germani Corporis Custodes*) were in effect a private force. Moreover, a number of inscriptions show that before the accession of Claudius in AD 41 individual members of the imperial family, and even one of Augustus' leading generals, Statilius Taurus, had their own German guards. The emperor's Germans appear to have been drawn originally from Batavian tribesmen from the Lower Rhine who were serving with the armies of Octavian when he was *triumvir*. Batavians and Ubii from further down the Rhine are the tribesmen who most often appear in the funerary inscriptions from Rome. Recruitment continued to be direct from Germany and Gaul, and inscriptions show that the individuals did not become Roman citizens. This was true of their officers also, although literary sources show both Caligula (AD 37–41) and Nero (AD 54–68) employing former gladiators in this capacity. The use of Germans, with their shaggy beards, immense size and renowned ferocity, was intended to discourage assassins.

The Germans acted as infantry when on guard at the palace but as cavalry in the field, and were always closely associated with the Praetorians. They were, however, para-military rather than a genuine part of the Roman army. Even so, they were organised in some ways like a regular auxiliary unit from an early date. Inscriptions show that they had officers called *decuriones*, like other cavalry, but that these commanded *decuriae*, probably of 30 men each, rather than *turmae*. One inscription also mentions an *optio*, an infantry rank, probably indicating the second-in-command of a *decuria*. We have no idea of how many *decuriae* there were – it probably varied – but the eventual designation of the Germans as a *cohors* on a coin of Nero suggests some sort of parity with the Praetorian Cohorts, probably at about 500 men. Suetonius reveals that under the same emperor they had their own camp 'next to the Gardens of Cn. Dolabella', possibly across the River Tiber where their cemetery lay. It does not appear, however, that the Germans had their own overall commander. Rather, the decurions may have taken charge of the watches at the palace and in the camp in rotation.

After accompanying Drusus to Pannonia, they are next heard of in AD 39 when Caligula supposedly received an oracle telling him to recruit more men for his 'unit of Batavians'. This provided him with an excuse for a visit to Germany during which he put down a conspiracy by the local commander, Gaetulicus. Be that as it may, when Caligula was assassinated by Praetorians in 41 it was the Germans who went through the palace looking for the murderers; they were also employed by Nero to hunt down the members of the Pisonian conspiracy in 65. Their long record of loyalty to their employers came to an end in 68 when, along with the Praetorians, they abandoned Nero in the face of Galba's uprising. Their reward was to be dismissed by the new emperor under suspicion of favouring another pretender. They may have met their end two years later as the bodyguard of the German rebel Civilis. The idea that they were reconstituted by the Flavian emperors in the latter part of the 1st century is based on a single inscription of doubtful relevance.

FROM VITELLIUS TO HADRIAN

(Sources: Pliny *Panegyric*; Suetonius *Lives* of Vespasian, Titus, Domitian; Cassius Dio LXV–LXIX)

The 'Year of the Four Emperors' ushered in a new dynasty, the Flavians, to replace the Julio-Claudians. Vitellius' Guard was merged with Flavian troops and trimmed down to nine cohorts. The Praetorian Camp was repaired and the new Emperor Vespasian's son and heir Titus was made Praetorian Prefect. Thereafter, the prefecture became the most senior post on the equestrian ladder. The Praetorians remained fiercely loyal to the dynasty. After Titus' brief reign (AD 79–81), his brother Domitian (AD 81–96) increased the number of cohorts to ten. In the mid-80s AD the Praetorians saw heavy fighting in Germany, and on the Danube against the Dacians, and in 87 the Praetorian Prefect, Cornelius Fuscus, was defeated and killed. When Domitian was assassinated in 96 the Praetorians felt aggrieved.

They vented their anger on the new emperor, Marcus Cocceius Nerva, the choice of the Senate. Nerva was a sinister character who had been involved in the suppression of the Pisonian conspiracy against Nero, and was probably implicated in Domitian's death. The Praetorians demanded the execution of one of their prefects, Petronius Secundus, who had been involved in the plot against Domitian, and Nerva abandoned Secundus to his fate. The emperor's situation was now critical, and he needed to adopt an heir who was in a position to avenge any move against himself. The strongest candidate was the governor of Upper Germany, Marcus Ulpius Traianus (Trajan), who could count on the support of eight German legions. On the death of Nerva early in 98, Trajan had the remaining Praetorian Prefect and his supporters executed. Trajan took his time about returning to Rome, possibly accompanied by the newly formed *Equites Singulares Augusti* (see below). He had already planned to deal with the Dacian problem by a major campaign across the Danube, one in which the disaffected Guard could play an important part and learn loyalty to their new master.

The Guard features prominently in the monuments to the two Dacian Wars which followed in AD 101/2 and 105/6, namely Trajan's Column and the Great Trajanic Frieze. This both reflects the importance of their role and acknowledges it publicly. The Guard also took part in Trajan's last campaign, the Parthian War (AD 113–7), which briefly extended the Roman Empire to its maximum limits.

The Imperial Horse Guards (*Equites Singulares Augusti*)[1]

By the early 2nd century the emperor had acquired a new cavalry escort in addition to the *speculatores* of the Guard. These were the Imperial Horse Guards (*Equites Singulares Augusti*), hand-picked troopers seconded from the auxiliary cavalry of the provinces, in particular those along the Rhine and Danube. They were evidently modelled on the units of individually picked men (*singulares*) who served as bodyguards to the provincial governors. There is some evidence from inscriptions to suggest that the Imperial Horse Guards were formed at the end of the 1st century and, although there is no certainty as to which emperor created the new unit, the balance of probability is that it was Trajan (AD 98–117).

The most plausible reason for the creation of the unit was the political situation surrounding Trajan's accession. As governor of Upper Germany, he had been adopted by Nerva in order to intimidate the rebellious Praetorians with the German armies. On

[1] See Speidel, 1965.

Trajan (AD 98–117) was governor of Upper Germany when he was adopted as heir to the throne by Nerva in 97 in order to counter the threat of insurrection by the Praetorians. He probably reformed his bodyguard from Germany into the Equites Singulares Augusti so as to have a loyal body of troops with him when he arrived in Rome. Soon afterwards he embarked upon the First Dacian War (AD 101–2) in which he made heavy use of the Guard in order to bind them to himself. (The Trustees of the British Museum)

Nerva's death less than a year later it would have made sense for Trajan to be accompanied to Rome by a force on whose loyalty he could rely. He already had *singulares* in his capacity as governor, and this is in itself an argument for assigning the new formation to him, since his immediate predecessors had not held a provincial governorship. It is quite likely that he simply took his German *singulares* with him.

Governors' *singulares* were seconded to the provincial capital for only about three years, and they remained on the books of their original units

throughout. During the Dacian Wars Trajan seems to have formed special scouting units in the same way. It is unlikely that individuals would have been re-equipped for their secondment, given that soldiers appear to have paid for and owned their own equipment. If so, such a unit would have presented a motley appearance – which would nevertheless have been a sign of elite status. Since they were only detached to an informal unit (*numerus*), troopers may even have retained their original shield blazons. The same would have been true of Trajan's *Equites Singulares*, at least initially.

The men seconded to Rome, unlike the provincial guards, did not return to their home bases but served out the balance of their term at the emperor's side. As the original draft retired they were replaced by fresh annual intakes sent from the provincial armies, and the *numerus* became permanent. Men were selected, probably by the provincial governor, after they had already served from three to seven years and proved their competence. They appear to have been granted Roman citizenship on transfer, without having to complete their 25 years like most other auxiliaries.

Although the *Equites Singulares Augusti* continued to be designated a *numerus*, they were organised and equipped in most ways like a regular cavalry unit (*ala*) and were housed in their own camp on the Caelian Hill. Overall command was in the hands of a tribune, although there are indications that he may have been in some way subject to the Praetorian Prefect. The tribune would normally go on to command an Urban and then a Praetorian Cohort, and the post was often given to high-fliers; a number of those recorded later became Praetorian Prefects. The unit was divided into *turmae*, probably about 30 men strong, each under a *decurio* with a *duplicarius* and a *sesquiplicarius* as his deputies; the senior decurion was designated *decurio princeps*.

A strength of up to 600 men is indicated by Hyginus' *On the Fortification of Camps* (chapters 7 & 30). This work, of disputed date between the late 1st and late 2nd centuries, gives instruction on how to lay out a temporary camp for an imperial expedition. It assumes the participation of 450 *Equites Singulares Augusti* camped alongside the emperor's tent, but also envisages the possibility of there being up to 600. Calculations from inscribed discharge lists, however,

suggest a strength nearer 1,000 men. Probably under Septimius Severus (AD 193–211), a new camp was built on the Caelian Hill to supplement the old one. Inscriptions suggest that it housed only about 500 men, and it is clear from a couple of military diplomas that these formed a separate *numerus* under their own tribune. This seems to indicate either that the original unit had been split in two, or that an extra unit had been added. Recruitment henceforth tended to be mainly from the Danube provinces, as with the Praetorians.

Singulares were often transferred as officers to cavalry units around the empire, so in this way the unit may have acted as an 'officer school' for the Roman army, but its primary function was to escort the emperor in the field. Presumably the *Equites Singulares* participated in Trajan's Dacian campaigns; it is known from inscriptions that they accompanied Hadrian to the Orient in 130, and fought for Septimius Severus at Lyon in 197 and in the East in 202. In all these instances they will have supplemented the Praetorians. Their close attendance on the emperor even in peacetime is implied by an incident recorded by Herodian, in which the Praetorian Prefect Cleander used them against protesters attempting to complain to Emperor Commodus at a villa outside Rome in 189.

The end of the *Equites Singulares Augusti* is obscure. They disappear from our view when inscriptional evidence dries up in the 260s, and they may not have survived into the 4th century.

THE 2ND AND 3RD CENTURIES

(Sources: Cassius Dio LXX–LXXX; Herodian; Historia Augusta *Lives*; Aurelius Victor *The Caesars* 28; 39; Zosimus *New History* I)

The wars of the late 1st to early 2nd centuries, and the renewed tendency for emperors to play a personal part in them, had made the Praetorians front-line troops and had turned them into a genuine fighting elite. They continued to fulfil this role for the rest of the 2nd century, which was in many ways their heyday. Praetorians accompanied Lucius Verus on

his Eastern Campaign of AD 162–6 and Marcus Aurelius in the North between 169–175 and 178–180. Two prefects were killed, and the prowess of the Guard is celebrated on Marcus' Column.

With the accession of Marcus' son Commodus in 180 and his withdrawal from active campaigning, the Guard were once again plunged into the political maelstrom. The Praetorian Prefect Perennis (AD 182–5) and the freedman Cleander (AD 186–9) exerted a great and malevolent influence over the weak emperor. Perennis fell when a delegation of 1,500 troops from Britain arrived in Rome to complain about his interference in the affairs of the province. Cleander used his influence to 'hire and

fire' prefects, sometimes on a daily basis. In 188 he obtained joint command of the Guard with the two prefects. It was Cleander who ordered a massacre of civilians by the *Equites Singulares Augusti* which resulted in a running battle with the Urban Cohorts. After Cleander's fall Commodus himself fell victim to a conspiracy led by his Praetorian Prefect Laetus on the last day of 192. The new Emperor Pertinax, who was in on the plot, paid the Praetorians a bonus of 3,000 denarii, but he only lasted three months before being murdered on 28 March 193 by a group of Guardsmen.

There followed one of the most notorious incidents in Roman history. The Guard put the Empire up for auction, supposedly conducting the bidding from the walls of their camp. The throne was eventually 'bought' by a senator named Didius Julianus. However, the Danube armies had already chosen as emperor the governor of Pannonia Superior, Lucius Septimius Severus, who besieged Rome and tricked the Praetorians into coming out unarmed. The Guard was disbanded and replaced by men transferred from Severus' own army. Once again the reign was plagued by the influence of a strong prefect, Plautianus, until his fall in AD 205. Nevertheless, Severus' new Guard fought with distinction against his rival Clodius Albinus at the Battle of Lyon in 197, and subsequently accompanied Severus to the East from 197 to 202, and to Britain from 208 until his death at York in 211.

Severus' son Caracalla lost favour with his troops by murdering his own brother and fellow-emperor Geta soon after his succession. He caused further problems by attempting to recreate an old-fashioned Macedonian phalanx in the Roman army. Eventually, in 217, whilst on campaign in the East, he was assassinated at the behest of his Praetorian Prefect Macrinus. This man then became emperor himself for a year before succumbing to the forces of Elagabalus, the great-nephew of Severus' formidable wife Julia Domna. The Praetorians objected to this priest of the oriental cult of Elagabal, and replaced him with his cousin, the 13-year-old Severus Alexander, in 222. For the first part of his reign the Guard ran out of control and did as they wished in Rome. At this period the Praetorian Prefect was taking on more and more of the general administration of Italy and there was a tendency to appoint jurists to the post, such as Papimian, who had held the prefecture from 203 until his removal and execution on the accession of Caracalla. Under Alexander the prefecture was held by the lawyer Ulpian until he was murdered by the Guard in the presence of the emperor himself. Another object of the Praetorians' displeasure was the emperor's guardian Cassius Dio, who nevertheless survived to write the history which is our best source for this period.

With the murder of Alexander in 235 and the end of the Severan dynasty, the Empire entered into a phase of anarchy; barbarian pressure on the northern frontiers increased, but one general after another used his troops to seize the throne rather than fight the enemy. In 238, with the bulk of the Guard away on campaign, the skeleton garrison of the Praetorian Camp was besieged by a crowd of civilians egged on by senators wishing to take revenge for the tyranny of the Praetorians. Meanwhile, the Emperor Maximinus' failure to bring the civil war against the pretender Gordian to an end led to his death at the hands of his own troops, including the enraged Praetorians. The senatorial nominees for the throne, Pupienus and Balbinus, recalled the Guard to Rome only to find themselves besieged by them, and they were both killed.

There is a marked deterioration in the conduct of the Guard from the time of Marcus. It is too simple to attribute this to changes in recruitment introduced by Septimius Severus. Rather, it was the result of chaotic conditions brought about by unbearable pressure on the frontiers coupled with a succession of flawed emperors who could not exercise control. It is hard to imagine that the Praetorians' involvement in politics at Rome did not affect their discipline and effectiveness.

After AD 238 both the literary and the epigraphic sources tend to dry up, and information about the Praetorians becomes scarce. In 249 they murdered the son of the Emperor Philip in the Camp. Under the Emperor Aurelian (AD 270–5) they took part in an expedition against Palmyra. In 297 they went to Africa with Maximian. Finally, Diocletian (AD 284–305) is said to have reduced the size of the Guard.

The end of the Praetorian Guard

(Sources: *CIL* VIII 9356; Nazarius *Panegyric to Constantine*; Eusebius *Life of Constantine*; *History of the Church* IX 9; Aurelius Victor *The Caesars* XL; Zosimus *New History* II 16)

In the end, perhaps unexpectedly, the Praetorian Guard went out in a blaze of glory. In AD 305 the two senior Tetrarchic emperors, Diocletian and Maximian, retired – a unique achievement – and the Caesars Galerius and Constantius were promoted. Constantius died at York in the following year, however, and the army in Britain proclaimed his son Constantine emperor. The Guard in Rome then made its last emperor by elevating Maximian's son Maxentius. A persecutor of the Christians, he is said

Maxentius (AD 306–12), the son of Diocletian's colleague Maximian, was made emperor by the Praetorians in response to the elevation of Constantine by the army of Britain. The Praetorians stood by him when Constantine eventually invaded Italy in 312, and they died with him in the Tiber at the Battle of the Milvian Bridge. Cast of the Torlonia Museum bust in the Museo della Civiltà Romana, Rome.

Above: Constantine the Great (AD 306–37), who defeated the Praetorians at the Milvian Bridge, and then disbanded them and demolished their Camp. He replaced them with his own guards, the Scholae Palatinae. Monumental head in the Vatican Museum. (German Archaeological Institute)

The strip relief on the Arch of Constantine in Rome showing the destruction of the Praetorians at the Battle of the Milvian Bridge on 28 October AD 312. The round panels above the relief are reused Trajanic pieces.

to have allowed the Guard to carry out massacres. Surrounded by rivals, Maxentius nevertheless held out, and his Praetorian Prefect defeated the usurper Domitius Alexander in 311. Eventually, Constantine invaded Italy in 312 and defeated Maxentius' Prefect Pompeianus. Maxentius prepared to face him north of the Tiber on the approach to Rome. The sources are contradictory, but he seems to have built a pontoon bridge near to the stone Milvian Bridge, either because the latter was broken or because it was too narrow for a large army. A few of the sources indicate that the pontoon bridge was designed to be breakable as a trap for Constantine. At any rate, on 28 October Maxentius' army was defeated at Saxa Rubra further upstream by an army buoyed up by Constantine's vision of the famous 'chi-rho' symbol and a divine promise of victory. The Praetorians retreated to the bridges fighting, but as they were crossing the pontoon bridge it collapsed and they drowned. Maxentius himself was flung from his horse into the swollen stream and shared their fate.

It was the end of the Guard. Constantine disbanded the Praetorians and demolished the west wall of the Camp which lies within the Aurelianic Walls. He himself maintained his own guards units, largely recruited from Germanic troops and known as the *Scholae*. Curiously, the post of Praetorian Prefect survived to become the senior civilian office in the Empire, but it was no longer associated with military command. The Praetorians were never reformed.

The Milvian Bridge as it is today, looking upstream from the north-west. The paler stones round the arches and at the bases of the piers are Roman, dating back to the original construction in 109 BC. Most of the superstructure is Renaissance and modern, but the overall appearance of the bridge is little changed. Maxentius and the Praetorians perished when a pontoon bridge, probably moored just downstream of the stone bridge, collapsed under their weight.

UNIFORM AND EQUIPMENT

The appearance of the Praetorians undoubtedly changed in the course of their history, but it is somewhat misleading to speak of 'uniform' at any period, either in the Guard or in the Roman army in general. Some uniformity within units will have been imposed both by prevailing fashions and by the natural association of individual units with certain armourers. Studies over the last two decades have increasingly stressed the diversity which was possible. In particular, the examination of private funerary reliefs and the excavation of military sites has called into question the strict distinction in equipment between legionaries and auxiliaries which is suggested by Trajan's Column. It is becoming clearer, for instance, that some auxiliaries did have segmental armour (the so-called '*lorica segmentata*', an invented modern term) whilst some legionaries used either scale armour (the '*lorica squamata*'), or mail armour (the '*lorica hamata*'). The labelling of equipment with personal names, together with papyrus evidence for stoppages of pay for clothing and equipment, suggests soldiers owned what they wore and carried. The variety of materials and decoration found in individual pieces indicates further that they had discretion as to how much they spent. Certainly, whilst troops within any particular type of unit must have had similar weaponry, there seems to have been no attempt to enforce visual standardisation as might be expected in a modern army.

Some types of equipment have always been regarded as characteristic of the Guard, in particular the so-called 'Attic' helmet with bushy crest, and the oval shield. These appear in a famous relief now in the Louvre, Paris, which was once dated to the early 2nd century but is now recognised as coming from the Arch of Claudius erected in AD 51. Oval shields are also carried by Praetorians on the Cancellaria reliefs of the reign of Domitian (AD 81–96), and on the Columns of Antoninus Pius (AD 138–161) and Marcus Aurelius (AD 161–180). The Attic helmet is ubiquitous for both Praetorians and legionaries on all public monuments, including the Great Trajanic Frieze of the early 2nd century incorporated into the Arch of Constantine. The combination has been thought of as imparting a conscious archaic 'look' to the Praetorians, at least in their parade dress – something akin to the red tunics and bearskins of modern British Foot Guards, but recent research casts considerable doubt on this idea. It is far more likely that the Praetorians were equipped in a manner similar to their contemporaries in the legions.

Helmets

The Attic helmet, so frequently seen on public monuments, with its distinctive brow-plate and permanent crest, has always dominated the popular image of the Roman soldier, despite its almost total absence from both private relief sculpture and the archaeological record. Robinson was able to identify

A scene from the Barberini mosaic at Palestrina, showing soldiers by the Nile in Egypt in attendance on the future Emperor Augustus. The date of the work is disputed, and may be anything between the 1st and the 3rd centuries AD. The two soldiers in the foreground are identified as Praetorians by the anachronistic scorpion emblem on their shields. Their tunics and helmet-crests are white, the most direct evidence for the colour of Praetorian dress. (Museo Nazionale Archeologico Prenestino, Palestrina)

only a single brow-plate and a separate cheek-piece which might have come from Attic helmets amongst all the helmet equipment which he lists. Together with the evidence of Trajan's Column, this has long since led armour specialists to abandon all notions of its use by legionaries. Attic helmets appear to be an artistic motif in Greek art which is taken over on Roman state monuments as part of the common visual language for the depiction of soldiers. Such monuments cannot therefore be employed as evidence for the actual use of this form of helmet by the Roman army (Waurick 1983; 1988). Despite this, the belief that it was worn by Praetorians, at least as parade armour, has persisted.

We can be certain that early in their history the Praetorians were still using the Montefortino-style helmet normal in the legions of the Republic and early Empire. An early 1st century tombstone of a Praetorian from Aquileia is decorated with a relief of such a helmet together with an oval shield; and an actual example which belonged to a soldier of the Twelfth Urban Cohort, which was in origin probably a Praetorian unit, survives in the Vatican Museum.

There is also evidence that in the latter part of the 1st century AD Praetorians were equipped no differently from legionaries. Tacitus writes in his *Histories* of an incident which took place at the Second Battle of Bedriacum near Cremona in the civil war of AD 69. During a night action in which Emperor Otho's Praetorians were suffering greatly from a huge

The Louvre relief, now thought to be from the Arch of Claudius erected in AD 51, has been the most influential of all images of the Praetorian Guard. The lower half of the left-hand figure, portions of the middle two, and the heads of all three figures in the foreground are modern restorations. The Attic style helmets are almost certainly an artistic convention, but the eagle in the background may be a form of Praetorian standard. Louvre, Paris. (German Archaeological Institute)

catapult operated by the opposing Sixteenth Legion, two Guardsmen picked up a couple of shields from the enemy dead to disguise their identity. In this way they were able to get close enough to the artillery piece to hack through its rope springs before they themselves were cut down. The story implies that what distinguished the Praetorians from the legionaries was their shields or shield-blazons, whilst their helmets and other equipment were indistinguishable. Presumably both sides were wearing variants of the Imperial Gallic or Imperial Italic style helmets by now common throughout the legions.

Robinson tries to explain the Attic helmets shown on the Louvre relief and the Great Trajanic Frieze by suggesting that such helmets were 'issued to troops for triumphs and other great occasions'. Yet it is increasingly doubted that Roman troops in general ever had special 'parade' armour, and, as we have seen, emperors were normally careful not to have visibly armed troops on show in the city of Rome. We also know for certain from depictions and literary sources that troops who took part in triumphs wore only their belted tunics. The balance of probability is that the Praetorians never wore the Attic helmet except by artistic convention on Roman state monuments.

Shields

That the Praetorians used the oval shield early in their history is guaranteed by the tombstone from Aquileia mentioned above. The Louvre and Cancellaria reliefs suggest that they continued to do so at least into the reign of Domitian (AD 81–96). There is no traceable artistic convention on the shape of shields to cloud the issue. This has been taken to contrast with the rectangular *scutum* adopted universally by the legions in the first half of the 1st century. The distinction, however, is again far from clear-cut. A coin of Gaius Caligula (AD 37–41) already depicts Praetorians with the *scutum*, whilst some funerary reliefs of the 1st century show continued use of the oval shield by legionaries (Bishop and Coulston). On Trajan's Column variants of the *scutum*, some with curved sides, are used by both legionaries and Praetorians. A Trajanic relief from Pozzuoli, now in Philadelphia, shows a Praetorian carrying a *scutum* with curved sides and a straight top edge (Kähler). By the end of the 2nd century both public and private

monuments are showing a return to the oval shield for both legionaries and Praetorians, although a mid-3rd century example from Dura Europus proves that the rectangular *scutum* did survive. So, while the oval shield may have remained fashionable amongst the Praetorians for longer than amongst the legions in the 1st century, the evidence suggests that there was no exclusive use of either shield-shape. From the end of the 1st century, at least, Praetorians and legionaries appear to have used the same shield types.

Tunics

The *tunica* was the basic Roman male garment, worn by soldiers and civilians alike, although soldiers wore it short above the knee (see the commentary to Plate A). It is frequently assumed that the soldier's tunic was usually red. The only detailed investigation of

A sestertius *of Emperor Gaius Caligula issued AD 40–1. His head is shown on the obverse with the inscription* C(aius) Caesar Aug(ustus) Germanicus Pon(tifex) M(aximus) Tr(ibunicia) Pot(estate), *and on the reverse he addresses the Praetorians (*adlocu(tio) coh(ortium)*). They appear to wear Attic helmets, and carry rectangular shields. Visible above their heads are four eagle standards. On one surviving example of this* type the shield of the leading Guardsman is engraved with a scorpion. (The Trustees of the British Museum)

Trajan's Column in Rome, set up to mark the height of the hill cut away for Trajan's new forum complex and dedicated in AD 113. Its base was also intended to house Trajan's ashes, whilst the frieze, spiralling round the Column from bottom to top, celebrates Trajan's great victories in the two Dacian Wars (AD 101–2 and 105–6). The frieze has always been one of the principal sources of information about the Roman army. In recent years, however, its rigid distinction between Praetorians and legionaries on the one hand and auxiliaries on the other, and the general uniformity of the various types, have increasingly been recognised as artistic conventions.

the evidence from mosaics, wall-paintings, archaeological finds and written sources by Fuentes (see bibliography), has shown clearly that the normal colour was white or off-white, the colour of undyed wool. Where red tunics are depicted they appear to be worn by officers, probably centurions, who also have red helmet crests.

What little specific evidence there is for Praetorians indicates that this held true for them also. The main evidence consists of a scene on the famous Barberini mosaic from Palestrina, depicting two fully armed men identified as Praetorians by the scorpion blazon on their rectangular shields (see below). Both wear white tunics and white crests on their helmets. It has sometimes been suggested that white was the particular colour of Guards units because in the 4th century and later the emperor's personal bodyguard were known as the *candidati* ('the shining-whites'). But these men did not derive their name from their uniform, though there is every possibility that they wore white as a sort of visual pun on their name.

The Arch of Constantine in Rome, situated between the Forum and the Colosseum. It was erected in AD 315 to celebrate Constantine's ten years on *the throne. It is decorated both with reused sculptural reliefs, which include sections of the Great Trajanic Frieze depicting Praetorians and* *legionaries in battle, and with contemporary friezes honouring Constantine, including one depicting the Battle of the Milvian Bridge in AD 312.*

There were *candidati* in the Roman army from no later than the late 2nd century AD, as we know from numerous inscriptions. These were men marked out for promotion, in particular to centurion, and so were quite literally 'candidates'. The term was borrowed from Roman political life, where candidates for office would canvass in specially whitened togas. It would be wrong to see the white tunic as in any way special to the Praetorians.

Body armour and other equipment

There is nothing to suggest that the rest of the Praetorians' arms and equipment differed from that of the legions, and this is in accordance with the anecdote from Tacitus already cited. It is true that two of the figures on the Louvre relief wear muscled cuirasses not normally ascribed to ordinary legionaries, but the central figure is certainly a senior officer, possibly the Praetorian Prefect himself, as indicated by the specially tied band around the cuirass. The lower portion of the less elaborately cuirassed figure on the left is a modern restoration, and the original could have had the same sort of band to indicate, say, a tribune. The overtunic worn by the soldier on the right is of interest and is paralleled by one shown on a single Praetorian standard-bearer on Trajan's Column (Scene cvi), but it is impossible to say whether this was a distinctive feature of Praetorian dress.

Trajan's Column seems to make no distinction between Praetorian and legionary equipment, ascribing the *lorica segmentata* to both, whilst following a convention of distinguishing auxiliaries by their use of mail shirts. Praetorians and legionaries are armed identically with javelin and a sword worn on the right side, but, in contrast with the earlier period, no dagger. The Great Trajanic Frieze only distinguishes infantry, wearing the *lorica segmentata*, from cavalry wearing mail or scale shirts. The figures on the Cancellaria relief and the very similar depictions on the Trajanic reliefs from Pozzuoli all show men equipped with the standard Roman soldier's hooded cape (*paenula*) worn over a tunic, a military belt with strap, apron, and the usual hob-nailed sandals (*caligae*). In all these items of dress they are indistinguishable from contemporary legionaries shown on private monuments, although the context of the Cancellaria reliefs and the scorpion on the shield of one of the Pozzuoli figures guarantees them as Praetorians. The only unusual features are the head of the javelin carried by one of the Cancellaria figures, which is apparently weighted with a lead ball; and the open-toed, open-heeled socks worn under the *caligae* on the same relief (see Plate E).

The Praetorians on the base of the Column of Antoninus Pius still wear segmental armour with Attic helmets, though they now carry the oval shield (which also replaces the *scutum* on private legionary monuments at about this time). Only in the late 2nd and the 3rd centuries do we get an inkling that the Praetorians in particular may have favoured scale armour over other types. It has been suggested by some scholars that the Column of Marcus Aurelius and other reliefs of the period use this armour as a convention to distinguish Praetorians from legionaries. This interpretation relies on, and accords with, a passage by the historian Cassius Dio who mentions an incident in which Emperor Macrinus (AD 217–8) lightened his Praetorians for an imminent battle by divesting them of their scale cuirasses and curved shields. Dio was writing only a decade after the event, and was a senior senator who knew Macrinus personally. He would certainly have been familiar with the equipment of the Guard, and his precise reference to scale cuirasses must carry the greatest possible weight. It may be significant that a century later the relief from the Arch of Constantine which shows the destruction of Emperor Maxentius' Praetorians at the Battle of the Milvian Bridge distinguishes them from the troops of Constantine by showing them in scale armour. There is no doubt, however, that legionaries were also using scale as well as mail armour throughout this period (segmental cuirasses having apparently gone out of fashion towards the end of the 2nd century). Private monuments commemorating Praetorians follow the contemporary fashion for all troops of not showing men in armour at all, but dressed in cloak (*sagum*), tunic with a single broad belt, leggings, and shoes rather than sandals. The suggestion, based on this, that armour ceased to be worn altogether has now been convincingly refuted (Coulston 1990).

Cumulatively, the evidence all seems to indicate that despite the artistic convention of the Attic helmet, and despite possible preferences for the oval shield and scale armour at various periods, Praetorians could not be distinguished from legionaries by their equipment.

Distinctive dress and insignia

There were nevertheless certain items of dress and forms of insignia which were peculiar to the Guard. Most distinctive of all, perhaps, was the civilian toga worn whilst on duty at the palace and in the Capitol in the first two centuries AD (Tacitus *Annals* XVI 27; *Histories* I 38). The symbolism and political significance of this impractical form of dress has already been explained. It is a feature apparently unique to the Praetorians.

Less out-of-the-ordinary is the special form of standard used by the Praetorians. Literary sources (Tacitus *Histories* I 41; Herodian II 6.11; VIII 5.9) indicate that Praetorian standards had imperial portraits (*imagines*) attached to them, whereas the legions and auxiliaries seem for the most part to have had such *imagines* carried separately by special portrait-bearers (*imaginiferi*). Praetorian standards have therefore been identified on Trajan's Column and other reliefs from their display of such portraits along with military decorations – mainly diffferent types of crowns (von Domaszewski). Legionary standards, by contrast, tend to display only varying numbers of

A scene from Trajan's Column (Scene v) showing Praetorian standards and horns being carried across the Danube during the initial invasion of Dacia, AD 101. The standards are surmounted by a sculptural figure and an eagle, and include honorific crowns, name-plaques and two imperial imagines each. The horns are fitted with a decorative extension not shown elsewhere on the Column and probably not used in battle. The standard-bearers (signiferi) and horn-players (cornicines) have lionskin headdresses, and under their cloaks they wear mail shirts over their tunics. Like ordinary infantrymen, they wear the sword on the right. (German Archaeological Institute)

A standard of the Third Praetorian Cohort from the late 1st century funerary relief of Marcus Pompeius Asper found at Tuculum near Rome. The standard is surmounted by a civic crown over a crossbar with streamers, and includes an eagle inside a torc, three civic crowns, a winged genius (Victory?), a mural crown, two imperial imagines, *a plaque with a scorpion, and a label inscribed* Coh(ors) III Pr(aetoria). *On the shaft can be seen the two lifting handles and the iron shoe for fixing the standard in the ground. Palazzo Albani, Rome. (German Archaeological Institute)*

discs, possibly corresponding to the number of the legionary cohort to which they belong. These identifications are guaranteed by the two standards of the first type specifically labelled *Coh(ors) III Pr(aetoria)* which are depicted on the late 1st century monument of Marcus Pompeius Asper preserved in the Palazzo Albani at Rome (see Plate G). This allows us to be sure that Praetorians are being shown in certain places on Trajan's Column.

Interestingly, these standards are often surmounted by an eagle, usually seen as the particular symbol of the legion. In fact, eagles were used to decorate several Praetorian tombstones (e.g. *CIL* VI 2742; 37193) and also appear inscribed on the lead ball in the head of the javelin carried by one of the men shown on the Cancellaria relief. Simple eagle standards are shown both on a coin of Gaius Caligula (AD 37–41) which is specifically labelled as depicting the emperor addressing the Praetorian Cohorts, and behind the soldiers on the Louvre relief who have always been identified as Praetorians. It is possible, therefore, that the eagle was a Praetorian as well as a legionary symbol.

Praetorian standard-bearers, whilst they carry the small round shield and are otherwise equipped like legionary standard-bearers on the monuments, are nevertheless distinguished from them by wearing lion masks and pelts, as opposed to bearskins, over their helmets and down their backs.

Praetorian Cohorts also seem to have had, as one would expect, their own shield blazons, presumably different for each cohort in view of their origins as separate units. Two basic patterns recur on both the public and private monuments. One is the winged thunderbolt and lightning pattern, so familiar from legionary tombstones, which is depicted on the Louvre and the Cancellaria reliefs, Trajan's Column, and the private monument of a soldier of the Fifth Cohort (*CIL* VI 2572). The pattern on the Cancellaria shields also includes individual moon and star shapes, which may also be particular symbols of the Praetorians (see Plate E). Moons and stars appear on the monuments of soldiers of the Sixth and the Tenth Cohorts (*CIL* VI 2602; 2742). An anecdote told about Gaius Caligula by his biographer Suetonius points in the same direction. During Caligula's much-derided expedition to Germany in AD 39 he is said to have led a body of Praetorian cavalry across the Rhine to take

Soldiers clearing trees to build a road in the mountains on Trajan's Column (Scene xcii). They are identified as soldiers by their sandals (caligae), but are otherwise dressed only in the tunic. This is worn belted to hang above the knee and with the right shoulder exposed, indicating that the garment was normally fastened rather than sewn at this point. The tool being used to chop down the trees is the dolabra, one of the standard implements of the Roman army, which could also be used for stripping turf and, in an emergency, as a weapon. (German Archaeological Institute)

part in a staged skirmish. For their efforts he rewarded these troops with a newly devised decoration, the 'scouting crown' (*corona exploratoria*), almost certainly a pun on the name of his special cavalry guard, the *speculatores*, which also means 'scouts'; Suetonius describes the 'scouting crown' as being decorated with 'sun, moon and stars'.

The other pattern appears only on shields which can reasonably be inferred to belong to Praetorians, and therefore appears to be more specific to them. This is a swirling vine-tendril blazon which appears with minor variations on one of the shields of the Louvre relief, on the Pozzuoli relief in Philadelphia, on a shield carried by a Praetorian on the Great Trajanic Frieze, on the Praetorians' shields on the base of the Column of Antoninus Pius and, most significantly, on a shield shown slung from the horse of a cavalryman of the Eighth Cohort on his tombstone in Rome (*CIL* VI 2672).

The blazon on the Pozzuoli relief incorporates what is probably the most characteristic symbol of the Praetorians, the scorpion (see Plate I). The connection is made certain by the prominent display of a scorpion above the label of the Third Praetorian Cohort on the standard shown on the monument of Marcus Pompeius Asper mentioned above. We know that some of the particular symbols adopted by individual legions derived from the astrological birth-signs of their founders. For instance, Caesar's legions tended to have the symbol of the Bull (Taurus), while Augustan legions had the half-goat/half-fish Capricorn (Keppie, 205–12). On this analogy, the scorpion, which is a symbol not known to have been borne by any other unit of the Roman army, is almost certainly derived from the birth-sign of the Praetorians' second founder, Tiberius (Leander Touati, 55–6). It appears on an example of the coin showing Caligula addressing the Praetorians, on two of the shields on the Barberini mosaic from Palestrina, and on the helmet cheek-pieces of several of the soldiers of the Great Trajanic Frieze. This is the clearest confirmation that we are in these instances dealing with Praetorians. Most spectacularly of all, three large scorpions appear on the upper portion of the shield of a cavalryman from the Great Trajanic Frieze (see Plate H).

THE PLATES

In the following commentaries on the colour plates, the sources of the interpretations offered have been indicated wherever practicable. It would have been tedious, however, to give individual references to the three works most frequently used, whose influence pervades what follows even where I have taken issue with them. The evidence for the colouring of cloaks and tunics can be found in the comprehensive article by Fuentes (1987). Russell Robinson's book on *The Armour of Imperial Rome* (1975) remains fundamental, especially on helmets. Finally, the new synthesis on *Roman Military Equipment* (1993) by Bishop and Coulston, two scholars whose individual contributions to the subject in recent years have been unrivalled, can be consulted on all aspects; its bibliographies are invaluable.

A: Praetorian Guardsmen off duty (early 1st century AD)

Before the Guard was concentrated in the Praetorian Camp in AD 23, three cohorts were billeted in Rome and the rest around Italy. Off-duty Guardsmen would not have looked very different from the civilians who were their neighbours in the multistorey tenement blocks of Rome. The basic article of male clothing for both military and civilian use was the tunic (*tunica*) (see Plate A1). This was a sleeveless woollen garment made of two pieces of cloth sewn together. The seams were apparently left unsewn either side of the neck and held together instead by a bronze safety-pin (*fibula*) or the like. This is implied by a number of relief sculptures, including a scene of road-building on Trajan's Column which shows that the tunic could be pulled down on the right side so as to leave the shoulder and arm bare for hard physical

A soldier depicted on a late 1st century AD funerary relief from Camomile Street, London. He wears a hooded cape (paenula) with a scarf (focale) over his tunic, and has a sword suspended on his right side from a belt with a strap apron. In his left hand he holds a box of writing instruments, perhaps indicating that he is seconded to the governor of Britain's headquarters staff. The paenula is fastened to halfway down the chest with two circular button-and-loop fastenings and two toggles, one of which has been damaged on the stone. (Museum of London)

work. Unbelted, the tunic would reach to mid-calf, but it was usual to blouse it out over a belt worn at the waist. Civilians would thus adjust their garment to a little below the knee, but it was the mark of a soldier to wear it much higher, at mid-thigh level. Further adjustment was made by bunching a fold of material behind the neck and tying it with a leather thong. As already mentioned, the usual colour of tunic for common soldiers, including the Guard, appears to have been white or off-white.

Soldiers would also have been recognisable by their military belt (*balteus*, later known as a *cingulum militare*) and their hob-nailed sandals (*caligae*). Finds and tombstone reliefs show that in the first half of the 1st century AD it was usual to have two crossed belts, one to suspend the sword and the other the dagger. These belts were relatively narrow and were fitted with bronze buckles worn on the hip, with bronze plates all round (**A2**). The plates were sometimes decorated with blue-black niello inlay and often surfaced with tin. *Caligae* are well known from military tombstones and reliefs from throughout the Empire and many actual examples have survived on waterlogged sites. They consisted of a fretwork upper, an insole and a sole, and were studded with hobnails; the uppers were laced with a leather thong. These remained the standard form of military footwear for the first two centuries AD.

In bad weather, soldier and civilian would both wear a form of coarse woollen hooded cape known as a *paenula* (see **A2**). Depictions on mosaics and wall-paintings invariably indicate a yellow-brown colour. The body was cut from a single piece of cloth, to hang with a straight lower edge (although a curved hem has also been suggested); a pointed hood was sewn on separately. The *paenula* was fastened down the front, apparently to mid-chest level, by various means: the Cancellaria relief shows the two edges fastened flush, suggesting hook-and-eye fastenings on the inside, but a relief in the Museum of London shows two visible button-and-loop fastenings and two duffle-coat-like toggles, as shown here (Bishop 1983). Round buttons of this type have been found at Pompeii made out of bone, and toggles are likely to have been of the same material.

B: Praetorian Guardsman and Centurion in the field (early 1st century AD)

This scene depicts a centurion speaking with a young Guardsman inside the turf rampart and palisade of a temporary camp. The setting is the campaigns of Germanicus Caesar in Germany (AD 14–16). Their equipment conforms closely to that of the figures on the late 1st century BC 'Altar of Domitius Ahenobarbus' and to that found in the archaeological record for the early part of the 1st century AD.

Both wear variants of the bronze Montefortino type helmet ubiquitous at this period; that of the centurion (**B2**) has been tinned. Helmets are held in place by two chin straps, permanently attached to rings under the neck-guard at the back of the helmet; these straps come round and cross over under the jaw to be clipped onto projecting studs on each cheek-piece. The crests, fixed by a pin inserted into a hole in the top knob, are of horsehair, white in the case of the Guardsman and dyed red in the case of the centurion, as is the latter's tunic; the colours are indicated by the depictions of men and 'officers' on the Palestrina

A bronze Montefortino-type helmet of the late 1st century BC from Castellani. This type of helmet is characterised by its crest-knob, bulbous shape, neck-guard and hinged cheek-pieces (missing on this example). It is of the type which predominates in the archaeological record of the late Republic and early Empire. One is shown on an early funerary relief of a Praetorian from Aquileia, and a surviving example in the Vatican Museum is labelled as having belonged to a soldier of the Twelfth Urban Cohort. (Ashmolean Museum, Oxford)

mosaic (Fuentes). Over their tunics (and probably some form of padding) they wear iron mail shirts, known mainly from reliefs, which have detachable mail doubling to protect the shoulders. The doubling is fixed at the front by two studs and a curved, hinged fastener of iron or bronze, several examples of which have been excavated on military sites.

Each of the crossed belts carries a single weapon. The four attachment rings found on surviving scabbard fittings, together with two small buckles found together with a sword on the island of Delos, suggest that it was suspended from short leather buckled straps passing over the belt (B1). Tombstones show that ordinary soldiers would carry the sword on the right side, officers on the left. The dagger, carried on the opposite side to the sword, was suspended from the belt by straps attached to rings on the sheath (see A2). The Guardsman's sword is based on an example found in the Rhine at Mainz and has the tapering blade characteristic of the 'Mainz'

A section of the so-called 'Altar of Domitius Ahenobarbus' from Rome, which is one of our few pieces of representational evidence for the Roman soldier of the late Republic; its date is disputed, falling between the late 2nd and late 1st centuries BC. These figures and the other two infantrymen depicted on the monument appear to be wearing Montefortino-type helmets and mail shirts with shoulder doubling over their tunics. They have a single belt suspending the sword on the right side, and they carry a large oval shield with vertical central spine, similar to an example found in the Fayum, Egypt. Louvre, Paris. (German Archaeological Institute)

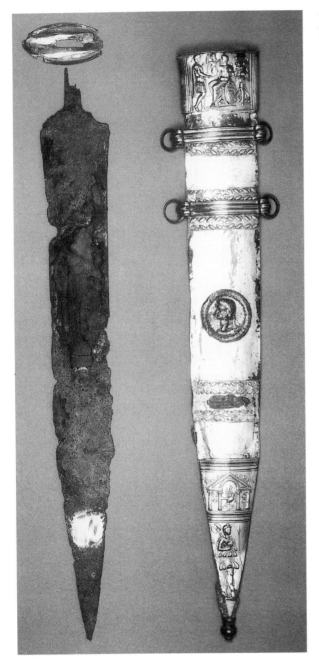

type, with a wooden pommel and hilt and a bone handgrip; the sheath has a bronze framework with perforated decoration over a leather-covered wooden lining. That of the centurion (B2) is based on an example found at Rheingonheim with a silver-cased wooden handle; the sheath is based on an early 1st century bronze sheath with embossed decoration found in the River Thames at Fulham. The men's daggers have riveted iron handles in two parts sandwiching the tang. The Guardsman's javelin is based on numerous examples from Germany and elsewhere; its long iron shank, riveted into the pyramidal head of the wooden shaft, was designed to buckle on impact should it miss its mark and stick in an enemy's shield.

The shields (*scuta*) are based on one found in the Fayum region of Egypt which corresponds to the type attested for the Guard at this period (see above), together with constructional details from the 3rd century *scutum* found at Dura-Europus in Syria. The Fayum shield was made of three-layered plywood covered with felt and had an ovoid wooden boss and vertical wooden spine on the outside. Polybius (VI 23), writing in the 2nd century BC, speaks of coverings of calf-skin over canvas, and the Dura *scutum* was likewise covered in leather, which is what is shown here. The edges have bronze binding of a type well known from military sites.

The centurion's rank is indicated, apart from by the colour of his crest and tunic, by his greaves (although these were not exclusive to centurions) and his vine-rod, as indicated on tombstones throughout the Empire. Depictions of Roman greaves and actual examples of cavalry 'sports' greaves show that they were bound on with straps or thongs rather than clipping on like their Greek predecessors; they were normally lined with leather. Literary sources and inscriptions indicate that the vine-rod was the special mark of the centurion and cavalry decurion.

C: Praetorian Guardsman, Emperor Claudius, and Praetorian Tribune at the Imperial Palace (AD 43–54)

A Praetorian stands on guard at the Imperial Palace on the Palatine Hill in Rome while his Emperor, Claudius, prepares to set off for a meeting of the Senate accompanied by the Praetorian tribune on duty.

The so-called 'Sword of Tiberius', a tapered-blade 'Mainz' type sword of the early 1st century AD, found by the Rhine at Mainz. This shape of sword is typical of the period, being replaced in the later part of the century by the parallel-bladed 'Pompeii' type. The richly embossed scabbard has caused this to be regarded as a special presentation sword because of its scene with the Emperor Tiberius and its supposed gold and silver decoration. Recent analysis by Klumbach has, however, shown that it is made of bronze over tinned bronze, which suggests that it was a relatively ordinary piece. (The Trustees of the British Museum)

Ironically, the most uniquely Praetorian form of dress in the early Empire was the civilian white toga which we know from literary texts was worn on duty, as a concession to the sensitivities of the Roman public. The toga had a variety of forms through Roman history (see Wilson 1924); but in the early Imperial period it was made of a single large piece of woollen cloth, one end of which was draped over the left shoulder and arm, and the other passed under the right arm and then over the left shoulder; the draping process had to be carried out with assistance. The toga was supposed to be held in place not by pins or brooches but by the clinging of the woollen cloth to itself (a toga made of smooth material would not stay in place), and by the holding up of the left forearm to provide support. Statues and reliefs often show the left hand gripping the fold of the toga at the left shoulder in order to rest the forearm. The toga was thus a relatively impractical garment, and, although the very symbol of Roman citizenship, it had, by the early 1st century AD, become highly formal and was usually worn only on special occasions; eventually, only senators wore the white toga regularly. Despite modern misconceptions of how Romans dressed, the use of the toga by the Praetorians when on guard at the palace or escorting the emperor to the Senate would have made them stand out rather than blend in with the civilian population.

The Guardsman (**C1**) is shown wearing his toga over the usual white tunic, like any civilian. The military *caligae* on his feet would, however, have given him away as a soldier, as would the bulge of the sword which we must presume he wore under his right arm (we have no descriptions or depictions). Since the sword was in any case drawn from a scabbard worn on the right side by pulling up and over with the reversed right hand, the toga ought not to have been too much of a hindrance. The tribune (**C3**) would as an officer, if he wore a sword at all, have carried it on his left side, whence it could have been drawn by the right hand from between the drapings of the toga.

The Emperor Claudius (**C2**) was already in his mid-fifties when he was unexpectedly elevated to the throne by the Praetorians after the assassination of Caligula. His biographer, Suetonius, tells us that he had a 'tall and well-built body, and was good-looking, with a fine head of white hair and a powerful neck, but

A figure from the Ara Pacis Augustae *(the Altar of the Augustan Peace), dedicated in Rome 9 BC. The man is generally identified as Lucius Domitius Ahenobarbus, a leading Augustan general and grandfather of the Emperor Nero. He wears over his tunic the woollen toga normal in the Julio-* *Claudian period, which was the attire of the Praetorians while on duty in Rome. He rests his left arm, which holds up the garment, by grasping the fold which passes over his left shoulder. His shoes are soft-leather* perones *with a single flap folded down at the front. (German Archaeological Institute)*

his weak thighs gave him trouble as he walked'. He is shown wearing the same sort of white toga as his Guardsmen and as any Roman was entitled to wear, since at this period it was still necessary to emphasise the emperor's position as being merely that of 'First Citizen' (*princeps*). Much later, emperors adopted gold-embroidered and even purple togas to mark their status. The frequent assumption that even at this period the emperor would have worn a purple stripe along the border of his toga, which was the mark of a senior magistrate in office, is unconfirmed by any evidence. Except on the rare occasions when the emperor held the consulship, he was not a magistrate, and it could be argued that the early emperors would have avoided the usurpation of a mark of honour to which they were not entitled and which would have irritated the Senate unnecessarily. He was, however, entitled to wear the broad purple stripe (*latus clavus*) of a senator over each shoulder of his tunic (that on the left shoulder normally being obscured by the toga), and the special senatorial boots (*calcei*) shown here. The latter were red or black and made of very soft leather, with bands wound round the ankle to mid-calf level; sometimes a crescent-shaped ivory toggle (*lunula*) was worn on the ankle as a special mark of nobility. These boots were worn with the toga only for sessions of the Senate (Talbert).

The tribune (**C3**) also wears his white toga over a tunic, but its purple stripe over each shoulder is the narrow one (*angusus clavus*) of a Roman knight (*eques*), to which order all Praetorian tribunes would belong. On his feet he wears the ordinary soft leather boots (*perones*) worn by senior officers. This type, often depicted on sculptural reliefs, including the Louvre relief from the Arch of Claudius, has the upper flap folded over and divided in two.

D: Bodyguard and Decurion of the German Bodyguard, reign of Nero (AD 54–68)

An ex-gladiator who has been appointed decurion of the German Bodyguard (*Germani Corporis Custodes*) berates one of his charges. The scene is set in the exercise yard (*palaestra*) of the baths complex in a town on the Bay of Naples, during one of the Emperor Nero's frequent visits to the area.

The appearance of the German Bodyguard is known to us entirely, but in some detail, from the reverse side of a single coin-type of the reign of Nero, which is thought to depict the emperor addressing his Germans. This is prompted by the fact that the soldiers are shown with swords and standards but without armour, and in particular by the heavy beards of two of the men, which was not the Italian fashion of the time and which suggests northern barbarians.

The tall, red-haired Guard (**D1**) wears the *paenula*, tunic and *caligae*, as shown on the coin. The tunic is hitched up on either side to reveal the upper thigh and produce a curved skirt. This was the military fashion of the middle part of the 1st century and is clearly depicted on the coin as well as on several

A sestertius of the Emperor Nero issued about AD 64–6. The obverse shows a bust of the emperor with the inscription Nero Claud(ius) Caes(ar) Aug(ustus) Ger(manicus) P(ontifex) M(aximus) Tr(ibunicia) P(otestate) Imp(erator) P(ater) P(atriae). *The reverse has a scene of the emperor, with an officer standing behind him, making a speech to some armed soldiers. This side is inscribed* s(enatus) c(onsulto) *('by decree of the Senate') and* adlocut(io) coh(ortium) *('address to the troops').*

The dress of the soldiers, consisting of paenula *and* tunic *rather than armour, and the beards worn by two of them, suggest that they are the German Bodyguard. (The Trustees of the British Museum)*

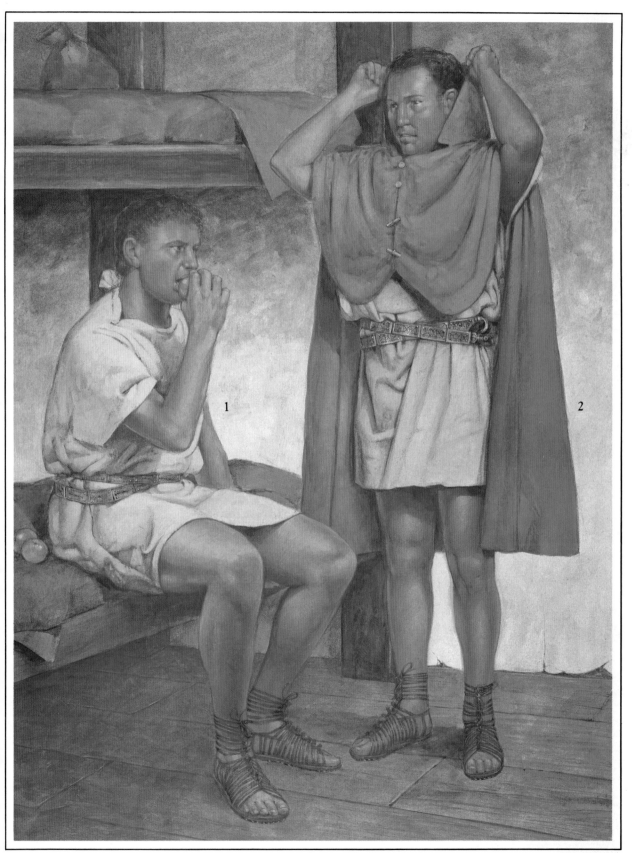

1,2: Praetorian guardsmen, off duty; early 1st C. AD   **A**

On campaign, early 1st C. AD
1: Praetorian guardsman
2: Praetorian centurion

B

On duty at the Imperial Palace; reign of Claudius
1: Praetorian guardsman
2: Emperor Claudius
3: Praetorian tribune

The German Bodyguard, reign of Nero
1: German guardsman
2: Decurion

D

Campaign dress,
reign of Domitian
1: Praetorian optio
2: Praetorian guardsman

E

The Third Praetorian Cohort, reign of Domitian
1: Signifer   2: Cornicen

F

Equites Singulares Augusti,
First Dacian War, AD 101/2
1: Trooper
2: Decurion
3: Trooper

The Praetorian Cavalry First During War. 2 10/6 1 V pillarion 3 Opti

Trajan's winter campaign on the lower Danube, First Dacian War
1: Praetorian tribune
2: Praetorian centurion
3: Praetorian guardsman

I

Trajan's winter campaign, First Dacian War   1: Praetorian Prefect   2: Emperor Trajan   3: Emperor's Lictor Proximus   4: General officer

J

1   2

The Praetorian camp, reign of Septimius Severus   1: Praetorian centurion, off duty   **K**
                                                                   2: Praetorian guardsman, on guard duty

The Milvian Bridge,
AD 312
1: Praetorian
guardsman
2: Emperor
Maxentius
3: Praetorian
tribune

L

legionary tombstones of the period. He wears crossed belts with bronze, niello-inlaid plates. These suspend on his left side a bronze-handled dagger and on his right a *gladius* of the 'Pompeii' type. This form of sword, with parallel edges to the blade, displaced the tapered 'Mainz' type in the latter part of the 1st century AD. The scabbard has a bronze chape and plates with incised and perforated decoration over leather-covered wooden boards.

The decurion (**D2**) conforms to the officer depicted on the coin standing behind the emperor (but without the helmet). He wears the military cloak (*sagum*) associated at this period with cavalrymen and officers. It is often shown on tombstones fastened round the neck with a circular brooch and decorated with fringes along the lower edge. The red colour of the cloak and tunic is suggested by mosaics and wall paintings for officers of this rank. The man on the coin appears to have a long cavalry sword (*spatha*) worn on the left side (the rank of *decurio*, attested by inscriptions for the officers of the Bodyguard, is in fact exclusive to the cavalry). The example shown has a silver-cased pommel and hilt and a scabbard of similar construction to that of the Guard's *gladius* with tinned bronze chape and plates. The single broad belt gradually replaced crossed twin belts in the course of the 1st century AD. The example shown bears the tinned bronze plates decorated with embossed roundels of the type which became popular in the latter part of that century and which adorned, for instance, the belts found with the skeleton of a soldier killed at Herculaneum by the eruption of Vesuvius in AD 79. The decurion also carries the vine-rod which is the mark of his rank.

E: Praetorian Optio *and Guardsman in the field, reign of Domitian (AD 81–96)*

A Praetorian *optio* (centurion's deputy) inspects a Guardsman about to mount guard in a temporary camp. In the background we see one of the eight-man leather tents used by troops on campaign. The setting is Domitian's wars on the Danube in the late 80s AD. The figures are equipped similarly to legionaries of the period and are partly based on the so-called Cancellaria relief, which depicts Praetorians accompanying the emperor as he returns from his campaign in Germany in AD 83.

Both men have helmets of the type classified as Imperial Italic D and E, examples of which were found in the Rhine at Mainz and at the fort at Hofheim in Germany respectively. Imperial Italic helmets were similar in many particulars to the better-known Imperial Gallic type but lacked the latter's characteristic embossed 'eyebrows' at the front or their decorative bronze bosses. They were normally of iron with bronze trim. Both types developed in the Augustan period and the basic form continued in use into the middle of the 2nd century AD. They were characterised by long neck-guards, often fitted with carrying handles for slinging the helmet when on the march, and by reinforcing peaks over the eyes. The cheek-pieces were tied at the chin and, in the case of the Imperial Italic type, the crown was fitted with a slotted box to take a twist-on crest support. The latter allowed the fixing of a painted wooden crest-box, which carried a horsehair or feather crest and was held in place by straps or thongs buckled or tied to rings attached at the front and back of the helmet-bowl. The rank of the *optio* (**E1**) is indicated by long feathers fitted in plume-tubes either side of the main crest. Several surviving helmets bear such tubes. He is also recognisable by the tall, knobbed stick he carries, which perhaps derives from his probable original function as rear officer of the hoplite phalanx, where such a stick could have been used to hold the line steady.

Under their *paenulae*, the men wear the segmental cuirass ('*lorica segmentata*'), developed in the early 1st century. It is conventionally used on Trajan's Column to designate Praetorians and legionaries, although the contemporary Adamklissi Monument and private tombstone reliefs of the 1st century show that both mail and scale cuirasses were also used by these troops. Segmental cuirasses were made up of individual, curved iron plates articulated with bronze hinges and leather straps; they were usually worn with a woollen scarf (*focale*) around the neck to prevent chafing. The cuirasses shown are based on an example found in a hoard of the early 2nd century from Corbridge.

The wearing of single waist belts is now normal. They continue to be decorated with bronze plates, which could be plain, inlaid with niello or embossed, and sometimes tinned. Moreover, in the course of the 1st century it became common for soldiers to hang an apron of up to eight leather strips from the front of

Left: A section of the Cancellaria relief, showing Praetorians accompanying the Emperor Domitian, probably on his victorious return from his German campaign of AD 83. The troops wear a scarf (focale) and the paenula over their tunics. Each carries a javelin and oval shield, apart from the emperor's spear-bearer on the left, who carries a small round shield under his left arm like a standard-bearer. The oval shields are decorated with a winged thunderbolt design supplemented by moons and stars which seem to be characteristic of the Guard. They also wear toeless and heelless woollen socks under their caligae. Vatican Museum. (German Archaeological Institute)

Right: A close-up of the head of the javelin carried by the right-hand soldier on the Cancellaria relief. Clearly visible are the binding of the shaft and the lead ball which weighted the head to add penetrative power. The latter is decorated with etched eagles. Vatican Museum (German Archaeological Institute)

Below: A close up of the right foot of the emperor's spear-bearer on the Cancellaria relief, showing the open-toed and open-heeled woollen sock worn under the caliga. This is the only surviving representation of such a sock. Vatican Museum. (German Archaeological Institute)

the belt. This would be decorated with bronze studs and weighted by bronze terminals which were again often tinned. Such an apron provided little protection but was perhaps worn for display. On tombstones it is sometimes shown tucked into the belt for convenience. By this period the waist belt is used for suspension of the dagger only, on the left side. The sword, still of 'Pompeii' type, is carried on the right side by a leather baldric slung across the body from the left shoulder.

The Cancellaria relief shows continued use of the oval shield of the earlier type (cf. Plate B) with ovoid boss, here hypothetically shown in iron with chased gold scorpion decoration, and a vertical spine in wood. The shield pattern shown, one of the few which can be associated with the Praetorians with any certainty, is taken from that relief. It incorporates the winged lightning bolts well known from depictions of legionary shield devices on Trajan's Column and tombstone reliefs, together with moons and stars. A shield with a lightning bolt device is shown on the monument of a cavalryman of the Fifth Praetorian Cohort (*CIL* VI 2572), and a moon and a star decorate another two funerary reliefs of men of the Sixth and Tenth Cohorts respectively (VI 2602; 2742). The colours of Praetorian shields are unknown, although reliefs show at most three different types of shield device in use by the Guard. The 4th century military writer Vegetius suggests, perhaps rather fancifully, that the cohorts of the legions before his time had been differentiated by the use of differing shield-blazons (*Epitome* II 18). Even if Vegetius is wrong about the legions, this is likely to have been true of the Praetorians whose cohorts were, in origin, independent units. If there was only a limited number of blazon types in use, then cohorts with similar devices most probably identified themselves by employing different colours.

The Guardsman's javelin (**E2**) is taken from the Cancellaria relief. Its head is weighted for extra penetration with a lead ball decorated with inscribed eagles, and it is fitted with a spiked butt. Another fascinating detail is uniquely illustrated by the same relief but confirmed by references in papyri from Egypt and in the Vindolanda writing-tablets. This is the wearing on occasion of socks inside the *caligae*, as depicted here. The socks are open-toed and without heels, but apparently with some form of binding round the ankle.

F: Standard-Bearer (Signifer) and Horn-Player (Cornicen) of the Third Praetorian Cohort in the field, reign of Domitian (AD 81–96)

A Praetorian standard-bearer (*signifer*) and horn-player (*cornicen*) signal an advance to men of the Third Cohort. Trajan's Column and other public monuments which depict battle scenes frequently show a close association between standard-bearers (*signiferi*) and horn-players (*cornicines*), who play the large, curved *cornu*. Vegetius also indicates that it is the sound of the *cornu* which signals the movement of the standards.

Trajan's Column follows a convention of distinguishing Praetorian and legionary standard-bearers and horn-players from the fighting troops by not depicting them in segmental armour, but instead giving them mail or sometimes scale shirts. These are worn in a variety of ways: over a very short tunic, over a normal-length tunic, and with or without a waist

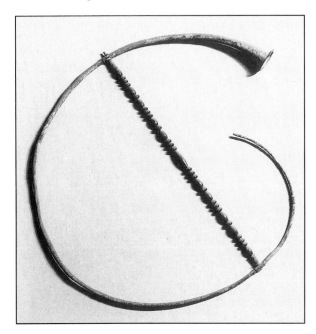

belt (sometimes with an apron). One of the Praetorian standard-bearers also has an overshirt covering the mail, rather like that of one of the soldiers on the Louvre relief from the Arch of Claudius. In all cases, unlike the fighting Praetorians and legionaries, breeches are worn to below the knee. It may be that these specialist troops tended, for purposes of easy recognition, to adopt armour which would make them stand out visually from their fellows. On the other hand, legionary tombstone reliefs do show such men wearing segmental armour without breeches, and the Cancellaria relief depicts the bearer of the emperor's lance of office carrying the small targe shield of a standard-bearer but likewise without breeches. The evidence, therefore, does not allow the formulation of hard-and-fast rules.

In this Plate the two men wear the Imperial Italic helmet (see also Plate E) and, over the tunic worn at its normal length, a dagged mail shirt ('*lorica hamata*') of the type most frequently depicted on Trajan's Column. As in most instances on the Column, a sword, of 'Pompeii' type, is worn on the right side suspended from a leather baldric across the body. As on the Cancellaria relief, they wear a waist belt with apron, and this suspends a dagger on the left side. Neither wears breeches, and one wears socks under his *caligae* (cf. Plate E).

Two pieces of equipment are certainly characteristic of these specialists: the small, round shield and the lionskin. The shields are borne by standard-bearers and musicians on the Cancellaria relief, occasionally on Trajan's Column, and on several tombstone reliefs. They are normally suspended on a baldric and, on the march, carried under the left arm, but a few tombstones show that they could also be slung over the back to release both hands. The shield on the Cancellaria relief has an all-over feather pattern that is of unknown significance. Animal skins are frequently shown worn over the helmet and down the back by these grades of troops, but whereas legionaries tend to have bearskins, both Trajan's Column and the Great Trajanic Frieze from the Arch of Constantine show Praetorians wearing feline pelts,

A bronze horn (cornu) of military type found at Pompeii. The horn consists of three main pieces connected by bronze junctions fitted into a (restored) wooden handle. The bronze mouthpiece is missing. Museo Archeologico Nazionale, Naples. (German Archaeological Institute)

and it is reasonable to suppose that this was peculiar to the Guard.

The standard shown (F1) is taken from two near-identical depictions on the funerary monument of Marcus Pompeius Asper, a former Praetorian centurion, which was found at Tusculum near Rome. These are invaluable, because the monument can be dated with reasonable certainty to around the late 1st century AD, and the standards are clearly labelled as being of the Third Praetorian Cohort. They thus provide our only certain picture of the form of Praetorian standards, which seem to differ from legionary standards in that the latter do not appear ever to have borne images (*imagines*) of the imperial family. The standard is decorated with silvered and gilt bronze plaques and figures, and consists, from the top down, of a silver spearhead, a civic crown of oak leaves, an iron cross-bar with leather streamers, an eagle within a torc, another civic crown, a figure of a winged deity (probably Victory), a mural crown, an image of the reigning Emperor Domitian (?), a plaque depicting a scorpion, a plaque with the inscription '*COH III PR*', a third civic crown, an image of the emperor's father Vespasian (?), and a fourth civic crown. The wooden shaft is fitted with an iron shoe for fixing in the ground and two iron handles to facilitate extraction.

The *cornu* (F2) is based on an example found at Pompeii. It is made of three main bronze pieces, with junctions into which the wooden handle is fitted, and with a bronze mouthpiece.

Cavalry scouts on Trajan's Column (Scene xxxvii) beckon to the emperor to advance during the winter campaign of AD 101/2. The men wear a scarf knotted around the neck, and a mail shirt dagged at the waist and shoulders over tunic and breeches. The long cavalry sword (spatha) is suspended from a baldric on the right side, and they carry an oval shield. The horses carry saddle-blankets and harness fitted with leaf-shaped pendants. (German Archaeological Institute)

A cavalry helmet of the mid-1st century AD found at Witcham Gravel, Ely, Cambridgeshire. The helmet consists of a bronze sheathing over an iron skull-cap. The sheathing is tinned on the crown, neck-guard and cheek-pieces and is decorated with bronze bosses. Scribed lines and six rivets on the crown reveal that it was originally fitted with a permanent crest-box. (The Trustees of the British Museum)

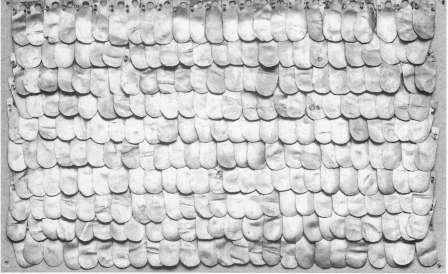

Bronze scales from Newstead, dated by their archaeological context to around AD 100. Each has four small side-link holes and one large hole at the top, probably for lacing to a foundation garment. These scales are relatively small, measuring some 2.9 cm by 1.2 cm, but others have been found as large as 8 cm by 5.4 cm. Shapes also vary: most are rounded as here, but others are pointed or even have a straight lower edge. The material can be either bronze or iron. (National Museum of Antiquities of Scotland, Edinburgh)

G: Troopers and Decurion of the Equites Singulares Augusti, *First Dacian War (AD 101/2)*

A trooper of the Emperor's Horse Guards (*Equites Singulares Augusti*) reports to his decurion during Trajan's First Dacian War, fought in what is today Romania. The trooper greets his officer with the cavalry salute of the extended right arm. The differing equipment and shield devices reflect the origins of the unit in troops seconded from the cavalry units of Upper Germany to serve as Trajan's cavalry guard when he was governor there only a few years before. Almost all of Trajan's Horse Guards would thus have been non-citizen auxiliaries recruited in Germany, whose equipment is known from extensive archaeological evidence as well as from private funerary reliefs. The hotch-potch appearance of such a unit would perhaps have been seen as the mark of a picked elite force.

The first trooper (**G1**) wears a helmet based on an example of the later 1st century found at Xanten in the Netherlands. It has a tinned bronze sheathing, decorated to resemble human hair circled by a laurel wreath, which covers an iron bowl, as is usual for

Silvered-bronze harness-fittings from Xanten in the Netherlands. The discs (phalerae) are backed with loops through which the leather harness-straps were passed. These are from a particularly fine set decorated with imperial busts and inlaid niello grapes and vine-leaves, closely dated to the late 40s or early 50s AD by the inscription Plinio Praefecto *on the topmost* phalera, *which reveals that the Elder Pliny was the contemporary unit commander. (The Trustees of the British Museum)*

51

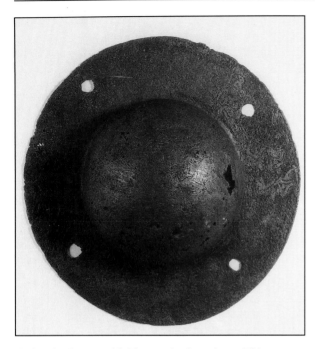

A circular bronze shield boss found at Kirkham in Lancashire. The boss would have been attached to a flat, oval shield board by four rivets. This example is decorated with incised military figures. (The Trustees of the British Museum)

cavalry helmets. He has a scale shirt with side slits, worn over a short leather shirt with strips (*pteryges*) attached at the shoulders, and a short woollen tunic. In addition he has a scarf tied around the neck in the auxiliary fashion, suede leather riding breeches worn to mid-calf, and spurs attached to his *caligae*. Suspended from a baldric across his right shoulder is a flat, oval shield of plywood covered in hide (although there is no direct evidence for leather facing on this type of shield); it is edged in bronze and reinforced by a metal bar running horizontally across the diameter. He is armed with a cavalry sword (*spatha*) suspended from a baldric on his right side and an ashen spear with iron head and butt. The feather tied to the spear is the mark of a courier (*pterophoros;* Plutarch, *Life of Otho* 4.2).

The decurion (**G2**) has a helmet sheathing based on one found at Ely in Cambridgeshire. It is of bronze with contrasting silver plating and is decorated with large bosses; the permanent crest-box is missing on the original but is clearly implied by the presence of scribe marks and six rivets on the skull (Robinson). His scale shirt is decorated by tinning of alternate bronze scales, as on an example from Ham

Hill. As marks of his rank, he wears his *spatha* on the left side and carries the vine-rod. The shield blazon is taken from that of an auxiliary trooper on Trajan's Column, as is that of the trooper who accompanies him.

The second trooper (**G3**) has a bronze helmet sheathing, again depicting human hair, of a type known from a fragmentary helmet found at Koblenz-Bubenheim as well as from several funerary reliefs. His mail shirt is based on those worn by troopers on Trajan's Column.

All three ride unshod horses of 14 to 15 hands with long manes and tails, of the type known from tombstones, public reliefs and horse burials (Hyland). The horse gear is typical of the late 1st/early 2nd century (Bishop 1988); this includes a padded leather saddle with four horns made by internal bronze stiffeners, which is strapped on through a woollen saddle-cloth. The leather straps and bridle are linked by niello-inlaid bronze, tinned-bronze or silver disc-junctions (*phalerae*). The decurion's horse also has a woollen neck strap and fringed breast band.

H: Flag-Bearer, Squadron Commander and Trooper of the Praetorian Cavalry, First Dacian War (AD 101/2)

A flag-bearer (*vexillarius*) of the Praetorian Cavalry (*Equites Praetoriani*) waits as a squadron commander (*optio*) prepares to lead his 30-man *turma* in a charge during the First Dacian War.

All three figures wear the Koblenz-Bubenheim style of helmet (cf. Plate G3) with an embossed scorpion on each cheek-piece. The *optio* (**H2**) is distinguished by the feathers fixed into plume holders either side of his helmet bowl. The men are all equipped with mail shirts and cavalry *spathae* worn on the right side, like the cavalrymen on Trajan's Column. The *optio* and the trooper (**H3**) carry in addition three short throwing spears, one ready to use in the right hand and two others held ready in the shield hand, as depicted on the monument of a contemporary cavalry scout, Tiberius Claudius Maximus (*AE* 1969/70 no.583). The horses are equipped in similar manner to those in Plate G.

The shields and the flag (*vexillum*) mark them as Praetorian cavalry. A hexagonal shield with this scorpion blazon is carried by a mail-shirted cavalryman on one of the panels of the Great Trajanic

Frieze; he can only be a Praetorian. Hexagonal shields are thought to have been of Germanic origin but are not infrequent on Roman cavalry tombstones. *Vexilla* are shown on both the Column and the Frieze

A Praetorian cavalryman on the Great Trajanic Frieze from the Arch of Constantine in Rome. He wears an Attic helmet, scarf and mail shirt, and he carries the hexagonal shield which is quite commonly used by cavalry troops. The horse-harness is decorated with ivy-leaf and lunate pendants. The shield blazon with three scorpions (presumably four overall) is unique but is clearly Praetorian. (German Archaeological Institute)

associated with cavalry, including men who can reasonably be identified as Praetorians. The Praetorian rank of *vexillarius* is attested by inscriptions. The form of the *vexillum* is based on numerous relief depictions and on a surviving example from Egypt, now in St Petersburg. It is a spear bearing a linen flag and studded leather streamers suspended from an iron crossbar; the Praetorian scorpion here replaces the 'Victory' emblem on the St Petersburg *vexillum*.

I: Praetorian Tribune, Centurion and Guardsman, First Dacian War (AD 101/2)

A Praetorian tribune receives a battlefield report from a centurion while a Guardsman looks on. The centurion gives his commander the infantry salute, raising the right hand to the helmet, palm inwards: this is shown on a number of reliefs, including the funerary monument of Flavius Mikkalus recently unearthed in Turkey.

The tribune (I1) wears the field uniform of a senior officer. The long cloak (*paludamentum*) is here fastened round the neck by a circular gold brooch, although several statues and private monuments show it fastened to the cuirass on the left shoulder and then wrapped trailing round the left arm. The colours of the cloak and tunic, white with a purple hem, are suggested by a wall-painting of the tribune Terentius of Cohors XX Palmyrenorum at Dura Europus in Syria. Our tribune also has a hinged iron muscle-cuirass bound round with a specially tied linen belt, as depicted on statues and monuments of several officers of this rank and above. The cuirass is always shown worn over a leather shirt with strips (*pteryges*) appearing at the shoulders and the waist. The wearing of woollen breeches with this uniform is unusual, but most senior officers on Trajan's Column have them, including the emperor. As a Roman knight, the tribune is entitled to wear a gold ring on his left hand. His military rank also gives him the right to carry a special dagger (*parazonium*) thrust into the linen belt, but with combat imminent he has swopped this for an officer's *spatha*, suspended from a baldric on his left side. In battle he would of course don a helmet.

The centurion (I2) is recognisable by his red crest worn transversely, as shown on two grave reliefs, his square red cloak (*sagum*) fixed by a brooch on his right shoulder, his red tunic, the leather shirt with *pteryges* worn under his cuirass, his sword worn on the left side, his greaves, and (obscured here) his vine-rod.

Whilst centurions may have continued to wear crests in battle for easy recognition (though this is only a guess), Trajan's Column and the Adamklissi Monument suggest that they were no longer worn by the rank and file. We do not in fact know when this change came about, since our last literary reference to the custom is by Caesar in the 50s BC (*Gallic War* II 21). Whilst 1st century helmets certainly had provision for crests, these need not have been worn in the field. The final abandonment of this type of crest may have been forced on the Roman army by the Dacian Wars. The Column, the Monument and a surviving example from Romania all indicate that helmets were being strengthened at this period with two iron crossbars over the bowl, blocking the crest-holder. A helmet from Israel of about 30 years later has this feature as an integral part of its construction, and

from the early 2nd century fittings for crest-holders disappear altogether. The change may have come about initially to counter the threat of the ferocious Dacian sickle-sword (*falx*), in parallel with the use of segmental arm protectors as depicted on the Adamklissi Monument (but not the Column). It is possible, however, that the Guard did not fit helmet crossbars in Dacia, since in one of the very few scenes showing the wearing of crests on Trajan's Column (Scene civ) the soldiers, depicted as listening to an address by the emperor, are clustered round Praetorian standards. Hence our Guardsman (I3) is shown with helmet uncrested but also unreinforced.

The Column also fails to show any soldier wearing a dagger, which may indicate that it was no longer the fashion to do so during the Dacian Wars. Continued finds of daggers, however, dating well into the 3rd century, show that this was not a universal change. Neither does the Column show troops who

Two cavalry flags (vexilla) shown on Trajan's Column (Scene vii). They each consist of a spear with crossbar and streamers, and a cloth flag with fringes. A surviving example of a vexillum with a Victory device was found in Egypt and is preserved in the Hermitage Museum in St Petersburg. (German Archaeological Institute)

The late 1st century BC funerary relief of the Appuleii from Mentana in Italy. The central figure represents the military tribune Lucius Appuleius in his officer's uniform; clearly visible is his cloak fastened on the left shoulder, and his officer's dagger. He holds the latter between the forefingers and thumb of his left hand at mid-chest level, presumably because it is pushed into the linen band round his cuirass. His knight's gold ring can be seen on the third finger. (German Archaeological Institute)

have segmental armour (i.e. legionaries and Praetorians) wearing breeches, but this is presumably only one of its conventions since the Adamklissi Monument does show this combination.

Finally, the rectangular shields with cut-off top and bottom and curved sides are based on a surviving relief (now in Philadelphia) from the lost Arch of Trajan at Pozzuoli (Kähler); Trajan's Column also depicts several shields of this general shape. The shield blazon with four spines and scrolled tendrils is based on the shield of a Praetorian from the Great Trajanic Frieze on the Arch of Constantine. A very similar design appears on the monument of a cavalryman of the Eighth Praetorian Cohort (*CIL* VI 2672) and also on the shield on the Philadelphia relief, which adds the scorpions to the design as shown.

J: Praetorian Prefect, Emperor Trajan with his Lictor Proximus, and General Officer, First Dacian War (AD 101/2)

The Emperor Trajan (**J3**), accompanied by his senior attendant (*lictor proximus*) (**J2**), discusses the campaign with his Praetorian Prefect, Marcus Claudius Livianus (**J1**), and his senior general, Lucius Licinius Sura (**J4**). The snow indicates that this is Trajan's campaign on the lower Danube during the winter of 101. The group is based on Scene civ of Trajan's

A dismounted cavalryman presenting a barbarian head to the Emperor Trajan on the Great Trajanic Frieze from the Arch of Constantine in Rome. He is identified as a Praetorian by a scorpion on the cheek-piece of his Attic helmet. (German Archaeological Institute)

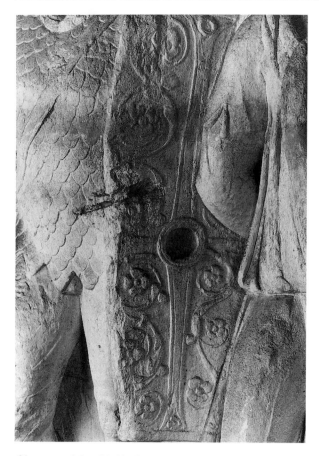

Close-up of the shield of the dismounted Praetorian cavalryman on the Great Trajanic Frieze. The blazon with spines and scrolled tendrils is similar to that of a cavalryman of the Eighth Praetorian Cohort (CIL VI 2672) and of the soldier on the Pozzuoli relief in Philadelphia (Kähler) which shows a horizontal scorpion device either side of the boss. (German Archaeological Institute)

Emperor Trajan (right) inspects a Dacian bow and arrow with two staff officers in attendance (Trajan's Column Scene xxv). All three figures are in identical general's uniform of a cloak (paludamentum), muscled cuirass with a linen band tied around it, leather shirt with strips (pteryges) hanging down, and a tunic; all of them also wear breeches. Since the reliefs would originally have been painted, the emperor was presumably differentiated by the purple colour of his cloak. The figure on the left is grasping his officer's dagger (parazonium) with the forefingers and thumb of his left hand. The figure in the middle is thought to represent Marcus Claudius Livianus, Trajan's Praetorian Prefect. (German Archaeological Institute)

Column which shows the emperor addressing the Praetorians.

All three of the main figures wear the senior officer's uniform (cf. the tribune in Plate I1). A long cloak (*paludamentum*) fastened with a brooch on the right shoulder is worn over a short iron muscle cuirass. The latter has a linen band tied around it, with a special knot at the front and the two ends tucked in; there is no evidence for the colour of the band. Under the cuirass is a leather shirt, with strips (*pteryges*) hanging down from the shoulders and the waist, and under that the usual tunic. They all wear fine woollen breeches and are shod with enclosed soft leather *perones* with lacing down the front.

Tucked into the linen band on the left side is the special senior officer's dagger, the *parazonium*. We know very little about this weapon or how it was carried. It is referred to in a short epigram by the poet Martial (XIV 32), and appears both on funerary monuments of men of the rank of tribune (Devijver) and on other reliefs showing senior officers, including the Column. A *parazonium* may be shown on the 'Altar of Domitius Ahenobarbus', implausibly suspended from one end of the linen band; but most other depictions suggest that it was carried at the level of the band, which is also indicated by its name.

The scene in the centre of the breastplate of the Prima Porta statue of Augustus. This depicts the future Emperor Tiberius, in general's uniform, receiving the return of a lost eagle from the Parthians in 20 BC. His *parazonium* is carried at mid-chest level, evidently thrust into the linen band round his cuirass, and he can be seen to be gripping the handle between the forefingers and thumb. Cast of the statue in the Museo della Civiltà Romana, Rome.

No distinction in dress can now be made out on the Column between the emperor and his generals, but the reliefs were probably in antiquity painted in bright colours, like most ancient sculpture; it therefore seems likely that, apart from the slight enlargement of his figure, Trajan would be recognisable from a distance by the colour of his *paludamentum*. The elder Pliny tells us that generals' cloaks were coloured scarlet with dye made from the kermes beetle (which he believed to be a berry). Livianus, the Praetorian Prefect, was a Roman knight, holding the most senior position available to members of the equestrian order; Sura was a senator and ex-consul, one of Trajan's closest confidants. Despite their

difference in status, their rank was comparable and so both probably wore the scarlet cloak. However, in the course of the 1st century, as the necessity to play down the true nature of imperial power diminished, emperors had taken to wearing a purple *paludamentum*. Eventually the garment, with its combination of military and regal overtones, became perhaps the most important mark of the imperial dignity.

The *lictor* (**J4**) carries one of the bundles of rods with an axe (*fasces*) which indicated power of command (*imperium*). The bundles could be untied and the rods used to beat wrongdoers; and the axe for execution, since *lictores* were the state executioners. The emperor was entitled to 24 such *fasces*, each carried by its own *lictor*, one of whom was designated as the senior or 'closest' (*proximus*). The linen ties of the *fasces* were scarlet-coloured (Ioannes Lydus, *On Powers* I 32), as was his cloak (Silius Italicus, *Punica* IX 420; Appian, *Libyca* 66). All the axes were decorated with small busts, some of them human, some of them animal. The figure shown is based on one of the *lictores* of the Cancellaria relief. *Lictores* were civilians, often former imperial slaves; consequently, under his *sagum* this man wears his tunic adjusted to hang just below the knees in the civilian manner. His boots are ordinary *perones* with a single flap folded forward.

K: Praetorian Centurion off duty and Guardsman on sentry duty at the Praetorian Camp in Rome, reign of Septimius Severus (AD 193–211)

An off-duty centurion of the Guard walks out of a gate of the Praetorian Camp (*Castra Praetoria*) past one of the sentries. The centurion (**K1**) wears the square red cloak (*sagum*) over a red tunic, which, as we know from private monuments, now has long sleeves and is being worn knee-length even by soldiers. A new style of broad leather belt has come into fashion. The tapering ends are passed through a large ring-buckle and clipped onto studs on the belt on either side. Woollen leggings have become normal wear and, in conjunction with these, *caligae* have been replaced by enclosed hobnailed boots, tied with integral leather laces which pass through eyelets cut into the leather. Several such boots have survived on waterlogged military sites in northern Europe. Although some centurions continued to carry a vine-rod, funerary reliefs show that others had adopted a stick with a mushroom-shaped head as a symbol of their authority.

The sentry (**K2**) has an iron helmet with large cheek-pieces and bronze fittings, based on an example found at Friedberg in Germany. Such helmets were once interpreted as cavalry equipment, but comparison with tombstone evidence suggests infantry use. The *paenula* has now been replaced by the *sagum* as the normal military cloak for all but senior officers. Wall paintings from Syria and Egypt suggest that it was usually yellow-brown or dark-brown. The white, long-sleeved tunic now has very narrow purple stripes over each shoulder, but these are of course obscured here by the cuirass.

The tendency of tombstones from this period onwards to show soldiers unarmoured has been shown to be an artistic convention, and it appears that armour was still worn in the 3rd century (Coulston 1990). This is guaranteed for the Guard by the notice of the contemporary historian Cassius Dio (78.37.4) that the Emperor Macrinus (AD 217–18) made his Praetorians more mobile for a specific engagement by taking away their scale armour and their dished shields, implying that this was a peculiarity: the passage implies that scale armour was usual for the Guard at this period.

The sentry's belt, baldric, sword and all the fittings are based on a complete assemblage that was found in a soldier's burial at Lyon, closely dated by accompanying coins to the very end of the 2nd century. The deceased may in fact have been killed at the great battle fought near Lyon in 197 in which Septimius Severus defeated his last rival for the imperial throne; he may even have been a Praetorian, since the Guard did take part in the battle. The long *spatha*, suspended on the left side from a baldric passing through a slide attached to the front of the scabbard, becomes universal at this period, even for common soldiers. The Lyon assemblage does not

A panel from a series of reliefs depicting the Emperor Marcus Aurelius (AD 161–80). The emperor, on horseback, and the soldier standing to the left of the panel, possibly a tribune of the Guard, both wear the senior officer's uniform. Both have parazonia *on their left side, apparently thrust into the linen band around the cuirass; that of the emperor is eagle-headed. The soldier to the right of the panel proferring a scroll to the emperor is probably a Praetorian. He wears a cloak (*sagum*) over a scale shirt and carries the oval shield which has now come back into fashion. Palazzo dei Conservatori, Rome (German Archaeological Institute)*

Soldiers setting fire to a barbarian village during the Marcomannic Wars, depicted on the Column of Marcus Aurelius in Rome. It has been suggested that the Column uses scale armour as a convention to distinguish Praetorians, in which case we might identify the central figure as such. He still wears a scarf, tunic, breeches and caligae; the sword is still suspended from a baldric on the right side and he carries an oval shield. Note that the wearing of beards is now the norm. (German Archaeological Institute)

include a dagger, but another contemporary historian, Herodian, mentions that Septimius Severus took away the belts and daggers of his predecessor's Praetorians when he reformed the Guard in 193; the wearing of daggers was therefore still the norm for Praetorians of this period.

Although the rectangular *scutum* did continue to be used in Roman armies, as shown by the 3rd century example found at Dura Europus, Praetorians are depicted with dished oval shields both on the base of the lost Column of Antoninus Pius (AD 138–61) and on the Column of Marcus Aurelius (AD 161–80). The shields found at Dura Europus suggest that by this period bronze edging had been replaced with rawhide sewn round the rim through holes in the board.

L: Emperor Maxentius with Praetorian Guardsman and Tribune at the Milvian Bridge (AD 312)

A Praetorian tribune gives orders to a Guardsman while the Emperor Maxentius looks on; it is late October of AD 312, and Maxentius is preparing to take his army north across the Tiber to meet the approaching army of his rival Constantine. To this end he has built a pontoon bridge alongside the narrow stone Milvian Bridge. In a few days' time he and his Praetorians will retreat across the pontoon bridge in confusion and be drowned when it collapses.

The figure of Maxentius (**L2**) is based on the sculptures of the four Tetrarchic emperors (AD 293–305) now in Venice (Delbrück). Although these sculptures are stylised, most of the details can be corroborated from artistic, literary, and archaeological sources (Alföldi). Maxentius wears a round leather cap, typical of officers of this period. Like earlier emperors he has a purple *paludamentum*, probably decorated with gold embroidery, as it certainly would have been later in the century. It is held in place on the right shoulder by a jewelled, golden 'crossbow' brooch of a shape typical of the late Empire. His tunic is of silk, with long rouched sleeves; it is decorated with purple and gold oval panels on the shoulders (which we cannot see) and with a gold-embroidered purple band along the lower hem. These details can be recognised on the relief of the Emperor Galerius (AD 305–11) on his Arch at Thessaloniki (Laubscher).

Over the tunic the emperor still wears the leather shirt with *pteryges* and the cuirass with linen band

A porphyry group of the four Tetrarchic emperors (AD 293–305) expressing their joint solidarity, now situated in St Mark's Square in Venice. The emperors are Diocletian, Maximian, Constantius and Galerius, the last two being shown here. These figures, some 1.3 metres high, would originally have formed the capital of a porphyry column like two which still survive intact in the Vatican library (Delbrück). The emperors are identically dressed in the leather pill-box hat worn by officers at this period – the holes were probably to hold metal wreaths, imperial cloak (paludamentum), muscled cuirass with jewelled band, leather shirt with strips, long-sleeved tunic, leggings, and jewelled shoes. Each carries a jewelled, eagle-headed sword, and a scabbard fitted with scabbard-slide and a chape with three domed rivets. (German Archaeological Institute)

Right: A detail from the frieze on the Arch of Constantine in Rome showing the final destruction of the Praetorians at the Battle of the Milvian Bridge on 28 October AD 312. The Guard use oval shields and can be recognised by their scale cuirasses. In accordance with artistic convention, they and the other troops on the relief still wear the archaeologically unattested 'Attic' helmet. (German Archaeological Institute)

worn by Roman generals since the Republic. The gilding of armour is now common, however, as we know from surviving helmets, and we can certainly assume that this would have been true of the emperor's cuirass. Indeed, Maxentius' opponent Constantine is described by Nazarius (*Panegyric* 29.5) as wearing a jewelled gold helmet and bearing a golden shield and armour at the Battle of the Milvian Bridge. The studding of equipment with jewels is also in fashion, as shown on the belts of the Venice Tetrarchs. The form of broad leather belt shown here, with its gold buckles and plates and its long tail hanging down by the right hip, is based on finds from Oudenburg in the Netherlands and depictions on reliefs and mosaics, in particular the contemporary hunt mosaic from Piazza Armerina. The suspension of the sword from a hip belt passing over the waist belt is suggested by several reliefs of the period. The details of the Tetrarchs' swords, including the jewelled scabbards, are entirely consistent with our other evidence. The eagle-headed pommel is a frequent imperial motif on reliefs and statues throughout the Roman period, and the scabbard slide for the hip belt is well attested archaeologically, as is

the scabbard chape with the three rivets. Even the purple leggings and purple leather shoes mounted with jewels and gold (*campagia*) can be corroborated from contemporary literary sources.

The tribune (L3) likewise still wears the traditional senior officer's uniform, although he cannot match the magnificence of his emperor. The Piazza Armerina hunt mosaic suggests that most cloaks were now yellowish-brown and marked with large purple oval patches decorated with white geometric designs (Carandini). The same mosaic, as well as frescoes from Egypt, show that his white woollen tunic also would have had purple oval patches on the shoulders and at thigh level and would have had purple stripes over each shoulder and purple bands on the cuffs. The red leather belt, of similar style to the emperor's but with the tail hanging by the left hip, is based on an assemblage found at Zengovarkarhony in Hungary. The 'propeller' stiffeners are particularly popular at this period, and the colour of the belt is suggested by several figures in the Piazza Armerina mosaic. The sword is based on an example with an ivory handle found at Cologne; the silver-gilt circular chape with niello inlay was found with the sword.

The tribune's finest piece of equipment is his 'Berkasovo' type helmet, with its silver-gilt sheathing, decorated with anchors for luck. It has a characteristic ridge, set over a ridged iron skull-cap with cheek-pieces. The helmet shown is based on an example found at Deurne in the Netherlands together with a coin-hoard which dates its deposition to around AD 319; similar examples found in Hungary are heavily jewelled. This was a new style of helmet, which was beginning to replace the cruder *spangelhelm*, i.e. segmental, type at just this time. James suggests this may have been the result of Diocletian's institution of state arms factories to improve army supply in the early 4th century.

The Guardsman (L1) has to make do with a crestless iron *spangelhelm*; his type of helmet had apparently been adopted in the latter half of the 3rd century, probably because of its cheapness. That shown is based on an example that was made from four plates joined by iron strips which was found in Egypt but is now in Leiden. Similar helmets are depicted on the Arch of Galerius. Over his white tunic, which would have had similar if less elaborate purple stripes and patches to that of the tribune, the Guardsman still wears the scale cuirass. Maxentius' Praetorians are specifically characterised by their scale armour in the relief on the Arch of Constantine which depicts their destruction at the Milvian Bridge. The Guardsman's shallowly dished oval shield of vertical poplar boards with sewn rawhide edging and horizontal stiffening-bar across the diameter, is based on examples found at Dura Europus. We have no information on Praetorian shield blazons at this period, but it is possible that some still incorporated the scorpion symbol, while the figure of Hercules, the patron deity of Maxentius' family who appears on one of the shields on the Arch of Galerius, was probably also used.

Bibliography

Collections of Inscriptions

AE   *L'Année Épigraphique* (Paris, 1888–)
CIL   *Corpus Inscriptionum Latinarum* (Berlin, 1863–)
ILS   *Inscriptiones Latinae Selectae* ed. H. Dessau, 2nd ed. (Berlin, 1954)

Modern Works

Alföldi, A. 'Insignien und Tracht der römischen Kaiser', *Mitteilungen des Deutschen Archäologischen Instituts. Romische Abteilung* 50 (1935) 1–171

Bellen, H. *Die germanische Leibwache der römische Kaiser des jülisch-claudischen Hauses* (Wiesbaden 1981)

Bishop, M.C. 'The Camomile Street soldier reconsidered', *Transactions of the London and Middlesex Archaeological Society* 34 (1983) 31–48

Bishop, M.C. 'Cavalry equipment of the Roman army in the first century AD' in Coulston (1988) 67–195

Bishop, M.C., & Coulston, J.C. *Roman Military Equipment* (London 1993)

Campbell, J.B. *The Emperor and the Roman Army* (Oxford 1984)

Carandini, et al., *Filosofiana. The Villa of Piazza Armerina. The image of a Roman aristocrat at the time of Constantine* (Palermo 1982)

Cichorius, C. *Die Reliefs der Traianssäule* (Berlin 1896–1900)

Clauss, M. *Untersuchungen zu den principales des römischen Heeres von Augustus bis Diokletian. Cornicularii, speculatores, frumentarii* (Bochum 1973)

Coarelli, F. 'L' "ara di Domizio Enobarbo" e la cultura artistica in Roma nel II secolo a.C.', *Dialoghi di Archeologia* 2 (1968) 302–68

Connolly, P. *Greece and Rome at War* (London 1981)

Coulston, J.C. (ed.) *Military Equipment and the Identity of Roman Soldiers. Proceedings of the Fourth Military Equipment Conference*, BAR International Series 394 (Oxford 1988)

Coulston, J.C. 'Later Roman Armour, 3rd–6th centuries AD', *Journal of Roman Military Equipment Studies* 1 (1990) 139–60

Dawson, M. (ed.) *Roman Military Equipment: the Accoutrements of War. Proceedings of the Third Military Equipment Research Seminar*, BAR International Series 336 (Oxford 1987)

Delbrück, R. *Antike Porphyrwerke* (Berlin 1932)

Devijver, H. 'T. Flavius Mikkalus, Ritteroffizier aus Perinthos', *Zeitschrift für Papyrologie und Epigraphik* 64 (1986) 253–6

Devijver, H. 'Equestrian Officers and their Monuments' in *The Equestrian Officers of the Roman Army* (Amsterdam 1989) 416–49

von Domaszewski, A. *Die Fahnen im römischen Heere* (Vienna 1885, reprinted in *Aufsätze zur römischen Heeresgeschichte* (Darmstadt 1972))

Durry, M. *Les cohortes prctoriennes* (Paris 1938)

Fuentes, N. 'The Roman Military Tunic' in Dawson (1987) 41–75

Frere, S., & Lepper, F. *Trajan's Column* (Gloucester 1988)

Heath, I. *The Armies and Enemies of Imperial Rome* (4th edn, Wargames Research Group 1981)

Howe, L.L. *The Praetorian Prefecture from Commodus to Diocletian* (Chicago 1942)

Hyland, A. *Equus. The Horse in the Roman World* (London 1990)

James, S. 'Evidence from Dura Europos for the origins of Late Roman helmets', *Syria* 63 (1986) 107–34

Kähler, H. 'Der Trajansbogen in Puteoli' in G.E. Mylonas (ed.) *Studies Presented to David Moore Robinson on his Seventieth Birthday* Vol. 1 (St Louis 1951) 430–9 and Pl.28

Kennedy, D.L. 'Some Observations on the Praetorian Guard', *Ancient Society* 9 (1978) 275–301

Keppie, L.J.F. *The Making of the Roman Army from Republic to Empire* (London 1984)

Laubscher, H.P. *Der Reliefschmuck der Galeriusbogens in Thessaloniki* (Berlin 1975)

Leander Touati, A-M. *The Great Trajanic Frieze. The study of a monument and of the mechanisms of message transmission in Roman art* (Stockholm)

Letta, C. 'Le imagines Caesarum di un praefectus castrorum Aegypti e l'XI coorte pretoria', *Athenaeum N.S.* 56 (1978) 3–19

L'Orange, H.P., & von Gerkan, A. *Der spätantike Bildschmuck des Konstantinsbogens* (Berlin 1939)

Magi, F. *I rilievi flavi del Palazzo della Cancelleria* (Rome 1945)

Maxfield, V.A. *The Military Decorations of the Roman Army* (London 1981)

Passerini, A. *Le coorti pretorie* (Rome 1939)

Petersen, E., et al. *Die Marcus-Säule auf der Piazza Colonna in Rom* (Monaco 1896)

Peterson, D. *The Roman Legions Recreated in Colour Photographs.* Europa Militaria Special No.2 (London 1992)

Richmond, I.A. 'The Relation of the Praetorian Camp to Aurelian's Wall of Rome', *Papers of the British School at Rome* 10 (1927) 12–22

Richmond, I.A. *Trajan's Army on Trajan's Column* (London 1982)

Robinson, H.R. *The Armour of Imperial Rome* (London 1975)

Speidel, M.P. *Die Equites Singulares Augusti: Begleittruppe der römischen Kaiser der zweiten und dritten Jahrhunderts* (Antiquitas I.11) (Bonn 1965)

Talbert, R.J.A. *The Senate of Imperial Rome* (Princeton 1984)

Watson, G.R. *The Roman Soldier* (London 1969)

Waurick, G. 'Untersuchungen zur historisierenden Rüstung in der römischen Kunst', *Jahrbuch des Römisch-Germanischen Zentralmuseums Mainz* 30 (1983) 265–301

Waurick, G. 'Römische Helme' in *Antike Helme,* Römisch-Germanisches Zentralmuseum Mainz Monograph 14 (Mainz 1988) 327–538

Webster, G. *The Roman Imperial Army* (3rd edn, London 1985)

Wilson, L. *The Roman Toga* (Baltimore 1924)

Wilson, L. *The Clothing of the Ancient Romans* (Baltimore 1938)

Notes sur les planches en couleurs

A L'analyse de toutes les informations existantes prouve que les soldats d'infanterie dans les légions, les auxiliaires et la Garde ont certainement porté une tunique blanche ou grège en laine brute. Leur cape pour temps froids (*paenula*) était boutonnée, crochetée ou fixée par des barrettes près de la poitrine seulement. Elle avait une capuche cousue et est souvent représentée en marron jaunâtre. La ceinture à plaques différenciait les soldats des civils. On en portait deux à cette époque. Les sandales à clous étaient également caractéristiques des militaires.

B Les campagnes de Germanicus, 14–16 av J.C. étaient réalisées par des soldats qui portaient encore le casque de bronze de type 'Montefortino' et l'armure en cotte de mailles. Le rouge semble avoir été la couleur distinctive des tuniques et des plumets des officiers si l'on en juge par la mosaïque de Palestrine. L'épée et le poignard de type 'Mainz' des soldats sont chacun soutenus par l'une des deux ceintures. Les centurions sont toujours représentés avec une épée à la hanche gauche alors que les soldats la portent sur la hanche droite. Les boucliers en contreplaqué, recouverts de cuir et bordés de bandes en bronze, sont inspirés d'un exemple et utilisent des techniques de construction de Fayum et de Dura-Europus respectivement.

C Lorsque la Garde était en fonction à cette époque, l'uniforme était la toge et seul le pommeau de l'épée et les sandales militaires révèlent que l'homme de gauche est un soldat. L'officier de droite, distingué par sa mince rayure pourpre qui indique sa classe sociale (un *eques* ou *chevalier*), porte sans doute son épée sur la hanche droite, complètement cachée. Il porte des chaussures de cuir souple (*perones*). Son empereur porte les *calcei* spéciales portées uniquement par les sénateurs. Claudius, qui aurait été semble-t-il bien moins handicapé que la littérature plus récente voudrait nous le faire croire, et qui est décrit par l'écrivain Suetonius comme grand et bien bâti bien que souffrant de faiblesse des jambes, porte seulement sa tunique sénatoriale avec une large bande pourpre qui le distingue.

D La barbe identifie, à cette date, un garde allemand barbare qui est ici insulté par l'un des ex-gladiateurs nommé comme officier de la Garde du corps allemande. Notez le style court de la tunique qui est remontée sous la ceinture pour former un ourlet courbé. Elle était spécifique aux soldats. L'épée 'Pompei' aux côtés parallèles apparut tard durant le 1er siècle de notre ère. Le décurion de droite porte le manteau

Farbtafeln

A Laut der verfügbaren Quellen ist anzunehmen, daß Soldaten ohne Rang in den Legionen, die Hilfstruppen und die Garde weiße, beziehungsweise grauweiße Tuniken aus ungebleichter Wolle trugen. Das Cape (*Paenula*) für kaltes Wetter wurde mit Knöpfen, Haken oder Knebeln nur an der Brust geschlossen; es hatte eine angenähte Kapuze und normalerweise eine gelbbraune Farbe. Der metallüberzogene Gürtel unterscheidet Soldaten von Zivilisten; zu dieser Zeit wurden zwei Gürtel getragen. Auch die mit Nägeln beschlagenen Sandalen sind charakteristisch für das Militär.

B Bei den Feldzügen des Germanicus, 14–16 n. Chr., trugen die Soldaten noch den bronzenen 'Montefortino'-Helm und Kettenpanzer. Nach dem Palestrina-Mosaik zu urteilen, scheint rot die kennzeichnende Farbe für die Tuniken und den Helmschmuck der Offiziere gewesen zu sein. Das Schwert des Typs 'Mainz' und der Dolch des Soldaten werden jeweils an einem der beiden Gürtel getragen; Zenturionen sind stets mit dem Schwert an der linken Hüfte abgebildet, Soldaten mit dem Schwert rechts. Die Sperrholz-Schilde, die mit Leder überzogen sind und eine Randeinfassung aus Bronze haben, sind jeweils einem Exemplar, beziehungsweise den Bauweisen von Fayum und Dura-Europus nachempfunden.

C Zu dieser Zeit trug die Garde im öffentlichen Leben die Toga, und lediglich der Schwertknauf und die Militärsandalen kennzeichnen den Mann auf der linken Seite als Soldaten. Der Offizier auf der rechten Seite, der durch den schmalen, violetten Rangstreifen (ein *Eques* oder *Ritter*) erkenntlich ist, trägt sein Schwert vermutlich gänzlich verborgen an der rechten Hüfte. Er trägt weiche Lederschuhe (*Perones*); sein Kaiser trägt die speziellen *Calcei*, die nur von Senatoren getragen wurden. Claudius – der scheinbar viel weniger behindert ist, als uns die spätere Literatur weismachen will, und der vom Schreiber Suetonius als hoch gewachsen und gut gebaut, jedoch mit schwachen Beinen, beschrieben wird – trägt lediglich seine Senatorentunika, die einen breiten Streifen hat, der ihn von anderen unterscheidet.

D Der Bart kennzeichnet zu dieser Zeit den barbarischen deutschen Gardisten, der hier von einem der ehemaligen Gladiatoren, die zu Offizieren der deutschen Leibwache ernannt worden waren, bestraft wird. Man beachte die kurze Form der Tunika, die in einer geschwungenen Linie unter den Gürtel gerafft wird, was den

sagum associé aux cavaliers et aux officiers, et souvent représenté avec des franges. Il a la longue épée *spatha* de cavalerie. La ceinture unique remplace à cette époque la paire de ceintures portée auparavant.

E *Optio* (distingué par une plume simple sur le côté et son bâton) garde du règne de Domitius en campagne, qui porte l'armure segmentaire de cette période. Leurs casques sont de type 'Italique impérial' avec un plumet monté sur une base en bois qui est lacée sur le casque lorsqu'ils sont en fonction. La ceinture à plaques qui soutient le poignard sur la hanche gauche du soldat, comprend également maintenant le tablier protecteur formé de lamelles cloutées. L'épée se balance maintenant d'une étroite écharpe. Le bas-relief 'Cancellaria', notre source principale, indique cette forme de bouclier. Nous ne connaissons pas les couleurs du bouclier du garde, mais le motif familier de l'éclair ailé avec des lunes et des étoiles se retrouve sur plusieurs pierres tombales de gardes. Notez le javelin *pilum* avec sa hampe plombée.

F L'étendard de la 3ème cohorte prétorienne est connu grâce à une sculpture funéraire. Notez la plaque représentant un scorpion. Le *scorpion* est un motif associé à la Garde depuis l'époque de Tiberius dont c'était le signe zodiacal. La cotte de mailles que l'on retrouve invariablement dans les sculptures des légionnaires et autres porte-étendards est portée ici, et notez les surcasques en forme de lion suggérés sur la colonne Trajane dans des sculptures que l'on pense représenter des porte-étendards et des trompettes prétoriens. De petits boucliers ronds sont portés sur le dos.

G Les *Equites Singulari Augusti* ou Gardes Impériaux Montés étaient une 'force' temporaire d'hommes recrutés dans d'autres unités. Ils portent donc diverses couleurs, ont divers motifs de boucliers et divers équipements. Le soldat de cavalerie donnant le salut de cavalerie en élevant le bras droit porte un casque 'Xanten', une cotte de mailles et un bouclier ovale plat. La plume attachée à sa lance indique un messager. Le décurion porte un casque 'Ely'. L'exemple retrouvé sur ce site portait en effet des marques d'une base de plumet attachée en permanence. Sur son armure à cotte de mailles, une écaille sur deux est étamée. Son bouclier et celui du soldat derrière lui vient de la colonne Trajane. Le second soldat porte la cotte de mailles et un casque de Koblenz-Bubenheim.

H Un *optio* (notez les plumes isolées) avec le porte-étendard de son escadron et un soldat de cavalerie, période de la guerre de Dacian. Ils portent tous des casques du type 'Koblenz-Bubenheim' avec des motifs de scorpions prétoriens sur les protège-joues. Ils portent tous la cotte de mailles et de longues épées de cavalerie. Notez trois lances à jeter portées par deux des cavaliers. Des vestiges de sculptures montrent le motif du bouclier à scorpions dans des contextes plausibles pour les *Equites Praetoriani*. Nous avons imaginé son utilisation sur le *vexillum*.

I Tribun prétorien, à gauche, en uniforme blanc d'officier supérieur et cuirasse moulante, avec longue cape *paludamentum*. Le centurion au centre fait un salut d'infanterie avec la paume tournée vers l'intérieur à la hauteur de son casque. Il porte encore le plumet transversal de son rang. Les soldats ordinaires semblent avoir abandonné le plumet à cette période, peut-être parce que les casques furent dotés de renforcements croisés qui rendaient difficile la fixation du plumet. La colonne Trajane montre une armure segmentaire, d'autres sources de la même période la montrent portée avec un pantalon court comme illustré ici. Le motif du bouclier provient de sculptures funéraires prétoriennes.

J Basé sur une scène de la colonne Trajane. L'empereur avec son *lictor* en chef (un esclave impérial et non pas un soldat) et deux officiers de haut rang. Les trois chefs portent une armure et un uniforme similaires mais nous avons imaginé que l'empereur aurait porté du pourpre et ses généraux de l'écarlate. Notez le gros poignard des chefs (*parazonium*), toujours sculpté dans une position suggérant qu'il aurait pu être glissé sous la bande de tissu attachée autour de l'armure du torse.

K Nous connaissons le costume très différent de la fin du 2ème siècle de notre ère grâce à des monuments. Notez la tunique à manches longues et les longs caleçons ou pantalons, la ceinture de cuir avec boucle et attachée par des clous, les bottines qui remplacent les sandales et le bâton à pommeau en champignon qui aurait peut-être remplacé le bâton de vigne traditionnel du centurion dans certains cas. Le casque de la sentinelle vient de Friedberg. On pensait que ces casques profonds et très protecteurs étaient du matériel de cavalerie mais on croit maintenant qu'ils étaient destinés à l'infanterie. Les sources littéraires confirment l'utilisation de l'armure à écailles. La ceinture et l'épée pendue d'une large écharpe décorée viennent de Lyon et sont datés avec précision. Les boucliers ovales semblent maintenant avoir remplacé le type rectangulaire dans toute l'armée mais pas complètement.

L La dernière image, encore une fois très différente de celles du début du Principat, montre l'Empereur Maxentius au pont Milvian. Notez la décoration de style oriental des costumes, le petit chapeau rond sans bord et l'utilisation des pierres précieuses. Le tribun, à droite, est copié de différentes mosaïques, fresques et trouvailles archéologiques. Son casque est du type 'Berkasovo'. Le garde discret à gauche a du matériel ordinaire et rudimentaire par contraste, inspiré de trouvailles archéologiques et de sculptures qui ont survécu.

Soldaten eigen war. Das parallelseitige 'Pompeji'-Schwert tauchte Ende des ersten Jahrhunderts n. Chr. auf. Der *Dekurio* auf der rechten Seite trägt den *Sagum*-Umhang, der Kavalleristen und Offizieren eigen ist und oft Fransen hat. Er hat ein langes *Spatha*-Kavallerieschwert; zu dieser Zeit wurden die paarweise getragenen Gürtel durch einen einzelnen ersetzt.

E *Optio* – durch die einzelnen Seitenfedern und den Stab zu erkennen – und Gardist der Herrschaftszeit des Domitianus auf dem Feldzug. Sie tragen die zeitgerechte Gliederrüstung. Ihre Helme entsprechen dem 'Imperial Italic'-Stil und haben einen Federschmuck, der im Dienst in an Ösen befestigten Holzgehäusen getragen wurde. Der metallüberzogene Gürtel, an dem der auf der linken Hüfte des Soldaten der Dolch festgemacht ist, weist nun auch den hängenden Schutzschurz aus genieteten Riemen auf. Das Schwert hängt nun an einem schmalen Gehenk. Unsere wichtigste Quelle, das 'Cancellaria'-Relief, zeigt diese Schildform. Die Farben der Schilde der Garde sind nicht bekannt, doch taucht das vertraute Motiv des geflügelten Blitzes mit zusätzlichen Monden und Sternen auf den Grabsteinen verschiedener Gardisten auf. Man beachte den Speer mit beschwertem Schaft.

F Die Standarte der 3. Prätorianischen Kohorte ist von einem gemeißelten Begräbnisbild bekannt; man beachte die Skorpionplatte – der Skorpion wurde der Garde als Motiv seit der Zeit des Tiberius beigegeben, dessen Sternzeichen er war. Der Schuppen- beziehungsweise Kettenpanzer, der auf Bildhauereien von Legions- und anderen Standartenträgern stets auftaucht, wird hier getragen; man beachte auch die Helmdecken mit dem Löwenkopf, die auf der Trajanssäule angedeutet sind. Man ist der Ansicht, daß die Meißelarbeiten prätorianische Standartenträger und Trompeter zeigen. Kleine, runde Schilde werden auf dem Rücken getragen.

G Bei den *Equites Singulari Augusti*, der kaiserlichen Reitergarde, handelte es sich um einen zeitweiligen 'Kampfverband' aus Männern, die aus anderen Einheiten eingezogen wurden. Es zeigt sich die Vielfalt an Farben, Schildmotiven und Ausrüstungen. Der Reiter, der den rechten Arm zum Kavallerie-Salut hebt, trägt einen 'Xanten'-Helm, Schuppenpanzer und einen flachen, ovalen Schild; die an seinen Speer gebundene Feder macht ihn als Boten erkenntlich. Der *Dekurio* trägt einen 'Ely'-Helm. Das an diesem Ort gefundene Exemplar zeigt die Spuren eines fest aufgesetzten Federschmuckhalters. Auf seinem Schuppenpanzer sind die Schuppen abwechselnd verzinnt. Sein Schild und der des Reiters hinter ihm sind der Trajanssäule nachempfunden. Der zweite Reiter trägt einen Kettenpanzer und einen Helm aus Koblenz-Bubenheim.

H Ein *Optio* – man beachte die einzelnen Helmfedern – mit dem Flaggenträger seiner Schwadron und einem Reiter zur Zeit des Dakienischen Krieges. Alle drei tragen Helme des 'Koblenz-Bubenheim'-Stils mit prätorianischen Skorpionmotiven auf den Backenstücken. Sie tragen Kettenpanzer und haben lange Kavallerieschwerter; man beachte bei zwei Reitern jeweils drei mitgeführte Wurfspieße. Überreste von Bildhauereien zeigen das Schildmotiv mit Skorpionen in Zusammenhängen, die für die *Equites Praetoriani* zuzutreffen scheinen. Wir halten den Einsatz auf dem *Vexillum* für wahrscheinlich.

I Prätorianischer Tribun auf der linken Seite in der weißen Uniform und dem Brustharnisch eines dienstälteren Offiziers mit langem *Paludamentum*-Umhang. Der Zenturio in der Mitte gibt den Infanterie-Salut mit der Handfläche nach innen in Helmhöhe. Er trägt noch den zuur aufgesetzten Helmschmuck seines Ranges; Soldaten ohne Rang scheinen zu dieser Zeit keinen Helmschmuck mehr zu tragen, was vielleicht darauf zurückzuführen ist, daß die Helme bald darauf durch Querstäbe verstärkt wurden, und die Befestigung des Helmschmucks hinderlich war. Auf der Trajanssäule sieht man Gliederpanzer; andere Quellen der Zeit zeigen ihn mit Kniehosen, wie das hier der Fall ist. Das Schildmotiv stammt von gemeißelten Begräbnisbildern der Prätorianer.

J Einer Szene auf der Trajanssäule nachempfunden; der Kaiser mit seinem leitenden *Lictor* – ein kaiserliche Sklave, kein Soldat – und zwei dienstälteren Offizieren. Die drei Befehlshaber tragen ähnliche Panzer und Uniformen, doch nehmen wir für den Kaiser die Farbe violett und für seine Generäle die Farbe scharlachrot an. Man beachte den speziellen, großen Dolch des dienstälteren Offiziers (*Parazonium*), der auf gemeißelten Abbildungen so dargestellt wird, daß man annehmen kann, er wurde in ein Stoffband gesteckt, das um den Brustharnisch gebunden wurde.

K Die recht unterschiedliche Bekleidung des späten 2. Jahrhundert n. Chr. ist durch Denkmäler überliefert. Man beachte die langärmelige Tunika und die langen Hosen; den Ledergürtel mit Ring und Knopf-Verschluß; die Stiefel anstelle von Sandalen; und den Stab mit pilzförmigem Kopf, der stellenweise den traditionellen Rebenstab des Zenturios ersetzte. Der Helm der Wache stammt aus Friedberg; solch tiefgezogene, umhüllende Helme schrieb man eher der Kavallerie zu, doch ist man inzwischen der Ansicht, daß sie zur Infanterieausrüstung gehörten. Literarische Quellen bestätigen den Schuppenpanzer. Der Gürtel und das Schwert, das an einem breiten, verzierten Gehenk befestigt ist, stammen aus Lyon und sind genau datiert. Ovale Schilde scheinen nun die rechteckige Form fast durchgehend ersetzt zu haben.

L Das letzte Bild, das sich wiederum stark von denen aus dem frühen Prinzipat unterscheidet, zeigt den Kaiser Maxentius an der Milvischen Brücke. Man beachte die Verzierung der Kleidung im östlichen Stil, den 'Pillbox'-Hut und den Schmuck. Die Darstellung des Tribuns auf der rechten Seite ist verschiedenen Mosaiken, Fresken und archäologischen Funden nachempfunden; bei seinem Helm handelt es sich um den sogenannten 'Berkasowo'-Typ. Der unscheinbare Gardist auf der linken Seite hat eine vergleichsweise billige und ungehobelte Ausrüstung, die aus archäologischen Funden und erhaltenen Bildhauereien überliefert ist.